Hangeul Calligraphy

Written by Gotdeul Lee Mi-Kyeong

Preface

Hangeul, the Korean alphabet, is a unique writing system in the world. It was created in 1443 by King Sejong of the Joseon dynasty (1392 – 1910), who invented and decreed the use of this new alphabet system. Hangeul was distinctly suited as a record of the Korean language as it was designed to perfectly represent the phonetic sounds of spoken speech. Nevertheless, its use was overshadowed by Hanmun, the Chinese character system, which had been the dominant official script for thousands of years. Thus, for hundreds of years Hangeul was primarily utilized by women, particularly royal and noble court members, who used it to record their lives and in their daily correspondence. As a result, the art of Hangeul calligraphy was developed by these pioneering court ladies, who invented its original style of writing with brush and Asian black ink. This classic style of Hangeul calligraphy is called 'Gungche' (palatial style).

The principles of Gungche calligraphy were researched and taught by two prominent women artists in South Korea. Galmul Lee Cheol-Kyeong (1914 – 1989) and her younger sister Gotdeul Lee Mi-Kyeong (1918 – 2022) were educated in Hangeul calligraphy from early childhood by their father Lee Man-Gyu, a Hangeul scholar and patriotic educator during the Japanese occupation of Korean peninsula (1910 – 1945). Afterwards, they established the Galmul Hangeul Calligraphy Association (1958) and helped promote Hangeul calligraphy as an official subject in the national school curriculum. They also instructed and mentored numerous professional calligraphy artists. In particular, the publication of a Gungche calligraphy textbook written by Lee Mi-Kyeong (1982) was instrumental in expediting the nationwide propagation of this traditional Korean art.

The recent advent of globalization in the 21st century has attracted a worldwide interest in Korean language and culture. Thus, the need for basic instruction textbooks of Hangeul calligraphy in foreign languages has also been widely recognized. Therefore, the English translation of Gotdeul's original Hangeul calligraphy textbook is the first step in an effort to meet such need. Though belated, I hope this book will be used by people around the world who cherish and enjoy the beauty of Hangeul.

In Translating Gotdeul's Hangeul Calligraphy

Traditionally, Hangeul has been written from top to bottom and right to left. Hanmun (Chinese script) has also been written in the same way for thousands of years. Top to bottom and right to left is the natural writing orientation in calligraphy as it follows the easy flow of brushstrokes. The original publication 'Hangeul Calligraphy written by Gotdeul Lee Mi-Kyeong' (1982) also adopted the same structure. Although this version chose to adopt left to right writing as default, illustrations and examples of calligraphic works from the original publication are kept as they are. Throughout this book, unique Hangeul words and concepts are introduced into English using the Revised Romanization of Korean, the current official system of spelling Korean into foreign languages (with a few exceptions due to conventions).

To translate the original text, this book attempts to use common English words as much as possible. However, readers are advised to pay attention to the meaning and usage of a few words. First, the word 'stroke' is used to indicate a wide range of calligraphic brushwork. However, *hoek*, the Korean word for stroke, is also used interchangeably as it is the core word in the original textbook and represents the soul of Hangeul calligraphy in general. Also, *hoek* is often conveniently used to refer to a continuous stroke composed of more than one line(s) or point(s). For instance, the second *hoek* of the consonant 'ㅁ' is a single combined stroke of both the top horizontal and right vertical lines made in succession while the first and third *hoek*s are the left vertical and the bottom horizontal lines, respectively. Second, the word 'line' is used to describe horizontal and vertical strokes in consonants such as 'ㄷ', 'ㄹ', 'ㅁ', 'ㅂ', 'ㅈ', 'ㅊ', 'ㅋ', 'ㅌ', 'ㅍ' and 'ㅎ' as well as those in vowels such as 'ㅡ' and 'ㅣ'. Occasionally, to indicate a line section of a multi-line stroke the word 'segment' is used. Third, the word 'point' is used to indicate short strokes – as in the short horizontal strokes in vowels such as 'ㅏ' and 'ㅓ', the top short strokes in consonants such as 'ㅈ' and 'ㅎ', but also the short vertical strokes in vowels such as 'ㅗ' and 'ㅛ', and short diagonal strokes (at the right corner) in consonants such as 'ㅅ', 'ㅈ' and 'ㅊ'. Fourth, the word 'node' refers to a configuration or joint between segments frequently created by pressing the brush tip during continuous writing, especially in the cursive form. The continuous writing of lines that make up a letter requires successive pauses and redirecting of the brush tip. These transition movements create pressed touches or accents, and these prominent stops become nodes. Fifth, when the brush tip first touches a given position on the paper, it is said to be 'placed', and when a now placed brush tip is subsequently used forcefully to give a stress, it is said to be 'pressed'. Each line may have a 'starting end/head', a middle, and a 'terminal end'. When the brush tip is 'lifted', it almost invariably means that the brush tip is still touching the paper. When brush is finally removed off the page, it is said to be 'released'.

This book is intended for those who want to learn the basic principles of Hangeul calligraphy. Those learning are advised to prepare *meokmul*, the Asian black ink, in the right consistency by finely grinding the solid ink stick against the surface of a *byeoru*, an inkstone (see p. 149). An adequately coated brush should be held with a relaxed hand while keeping an upright body posture, and placed perpendicular to the paper. Thus, unlike in painting, the use of a brush in calligraphy requires strict discipline and order. A horizontal line is written almost invariably from left to right, and vertical lines only from top to bottom. In this regard, the word 'draw' is not appropriate and so avoided to describe any calligraphic methods here. Finally, to help readers for whom literal translations of the original text may not be sufficient to articulate the author's instructions, additional explanations have been provided. Hopefully, these efforts will help enhance students' understanding of Hangeul calligraphy.

About Calligraphy Writing

The classic calligraphic works by old masters included for reference at the end of this book (pp. 144 – 145) show that single points and lines written with such care and devotion enables us to feel a sense of calmness and stability. *Gungche* calligraphy requires an artist's sincere mind. Therefore, prior to learning calligraphy, students must have their mindset prepared.

Foremost in importance is learning how to do basic *hoeks* (strokes). It can be compared to a carpenter's trimming and preparing of raw wood materials prior to making furniture. Just as finely hewn pieces of wood enable the crafting of beautiful objects while roughly prepared ones coarse, calligraphy pieces shine only when every *hoek* is good and solid.

The first stage of studying *hoek* brushwork is to learn basic brushstroke technique. Second, the direction of strokes must be correct; and third, the shape of the resulting strokes itself must be beautiful. Even when these conditions are met, the characteristic qualities of each point and line are not attained without sophisticated refinement. To reach such a level, repeated practice is required. Calligraphy should be studied with one's arms rather than eyes. Only when your arms move freely can your brushwork be handled freely, and *hoeks* made in this physical precondition become natural. Thus, students must practice brushstrokes *hoek* after *hoek* with great attention as many times as possible. After sufficient practice with *hoeks*, students can move on to the next stage of writing large characters. Although each character appears easy to shape at first glance, this stage requires plentiful practice too.

When each character is written satisfactorily, advance towards writing six characters on a single sheet of paper. Fold paper into six parts and practice how to write them together so that they fit with each other. Successful writing of single characters does not necessarily guarantee balanced writing of multiple characters. Practice is again needed to be able to write them harmoniously. Steady practice with six and eight characters by this method will help to write more characters with significantly less difficulty.

Gotdeul Lee Mi-Kyeong

4

Gotdeul[1] Lee Mi-Kyeong

1918 – 2022

Graduated from the Department of Music, Ewha College[2] in 1939

Calligraphy lecturer at Ewha Girls' Middle and High School, 1954 – 1963

Calligraphy lecturer at YWCA, 1970 – 1975

Calligraphy instructor at Galmul[3] Hangeul Calligraphy Association[4], 1971 – 1994

Member of the International Calligraphy Art Association, member of Cheonglimhoe

Guest artist of the Exhibition of Korean Contemporary Art (1978 – 1989)

Exhibition: Galmul and Gotdeul Sister Exhibition (Los Angeles, USA and Toronto, Canada, 1983), 70th Anniversary Exhibition (1987), 100th Anniversary Exhibition (2017)

Donation: 'Manpokdong Paldamga' (Seoul Arts Center, Seoul, Korea, 1988), 'Ohuhga' (Asian Art Museum, San Francisco, USA, 1993), 'Sagyejeolui Norae' (Seattle Art Museum, Seattle, USA, 1993), 'Mal Hanmadi' (Royal Ontario Museum, Toronto, Canada, 1994), 'Gwandongbyeolgok' (Ewha Womans University Museum, Seoul, Korea, 2000), 'Gwandongbyeolgok-eseo' (State Museum of Oriental Art, Moscow, Russia, 2005), 'Maehwasa' (National Hangeul Museum, Seoul, Korea, 2017)

Awards: Presidential Culture Award (2007), Korean Art Association Artist Award (2009)

Publication: 'Hangeul' (co-authored by Galmul and Gotdeul), 'Butkeutte Garak Sileo' (Tunes carried on brush tip; Gotdeul's *sijo* works)

---

[1] Gotdeul (flower garden; pronounced like 'kkot tteul') is the pen name of Lee Mi-Kyeong.

[2] Presently Ewha Womans University

[3] Galmul (autumn water) is the pen name of Lee Cheol-Kyeong, an elder sister of Lee Mi-Kyeong and a founder of Galmul Hangeul Calligraphy Association (1958).

[4] A leading organization of Hangeul calligraphers in Korea. Members aim to research and promote *Gungche*, a traditional Hangeul calligraphy style.

Contents

The Print Style

ㅣ

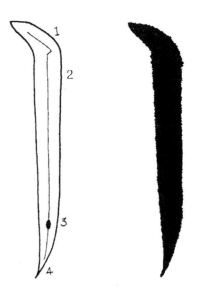

* ' ㅣ ' is the most basic *hoek* (line) in calligraphy. Beginners should learn to use the full tip of the brush to make a solid stroke while concentrating on keeping an upright body posture. Practicing it multiple times is advised.

1. Place the brush tip at an angle as shown and press it as if making a point.

2. Keeping the brush tip connected to paper, turn the tip downward and move it straight down slowly.

3. Approaching the end, pause brush momentarily, then move it further down while lifting the brush tip, drawing the hairs together. This helps thin out the terminal end of the line.

4. Release brush to the left, leaving a short pointed end.

ㅏ

After completing ' ㅣ ', place the brush tip at the position shown, slightly lower than the midpoint of ' ㅣ ', and lightly press it horizontally to the right. To finish the resulting point, press the brush tip downward as if letting it droop, then lift and release it to the left.

ㅑ

After completing ' ㅣ ', make two horizontal points to the right in equal shape and direction. Alternatively, make the upper point angled slightly upward and the lower one slightly downward.

ㅓ

To make the horizontal point first, gently place the brush tip and move it to the right in a slightly upward direction. Without pressing the brush tip too hard, lift and release it. To the right of the point, add 'ㅣ'. Unlike 'ㅏ', connect the point approximately at the midpoint of 'ㅣ'.

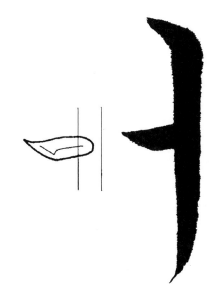

ㅕ

Make the upper point first. Place the brush tip gently to the right, move it with a slight upward slant as if rolling the brush hairs over, then lift and release it horizontally. For the lower point, place the brush tip lightly, move it to the right tilting slightly downward, and lift and release it horizontally. Afterwards, add 'ㅣ' to the right.

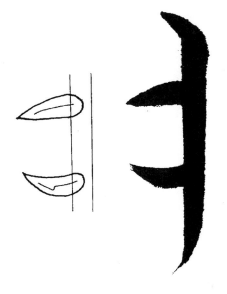

ㅡ

1. Place and press the brush tip horizontally to the right at the angle shown. Keeping the pressed brush tip touching the paper, adjust its direction by moving it upwards to raise the brush hairs upright. This creates the starting head of the *hoek*.

2. Move brush to the right slowly. Let the brush tip occupy the center of the horizontal line. Keep the resulting line straight slanting slightly upward.

3. Turn and press the brush tip to the right and downward, creating the terminal end of the *hoek*. Lift and release the brush tip towards the left.

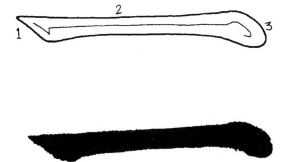

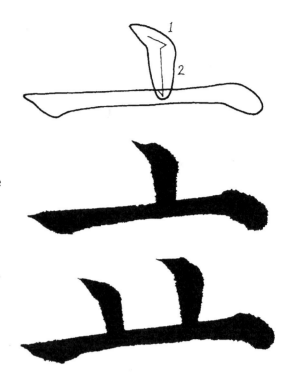

ㅗ ㅛ

1. To make a vertical point first, place the brush tip nearly horizontally and press it to the right in a downward direction. Keeping the brush tip connected, raise the tip hairs upright.

2. Turn the direction of the brush tip vertically and move it down. In the process lift the brush tip slightly to taper the bottom end. Complete the point by releasing the brush tip. Afterwards, add a horizontal line underneath.

* 'ㅛ' can be written by making two parallel vertical points, the left one first and the right one later. The right vertical point should be started at a slightly higher position than the left one. Add 'ㅡ' underneath. The two vertical points should be located at positions approximately one third and two thirds the length of the bottom horizontal line.

ㅜ ㅠ

* Make a horizontal line first. Then begin the vertical line(s) from inside of the *hoek* 'ㅡ'.

1. For the vertical line of 'ㅜ', place the brush tip nearly horizontally at a position approximately two thirds of the line from its starting end. Press the brush tip then raise the tip hairs up.

2. Roll the brush tip over and move it down vertically. This allows the brush tip to occupy the center of the line.

3. Pause the brush tip momentarily, draw the brush hairs together, then lift and release the brush tip by pulling it down briefly, leaving a short pointed end.

* For 'ㅠ', place the brush tip at positions approximately one third and two thirds on the line for the first (left) and second (right) vertical lines, respectively. The first vertical line bends towards the left, whereas the second one moves straight down a distance roughly equal to the height of the consonant placed at the top (when writing a full character). Note that the resulting second vertical line can be bent slightly to the right to counterbalance the leftward bent of the first vertical line.

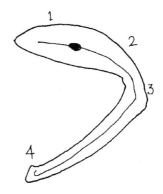

ㄱ (가 갸 거 겨 기)

1. Place the brush tip as if making a horizontal point. Press it towards the right.

2. Lift the brush tip and move it to the right in a slightly downward curve.

3. Raise the brush hairs, adjust the direction of the brush tip leftwards, and move it downward towards the left.

4. Approaching the end of the resulting diagonal segment, turn the brush tip horizontally, pause it calmly in a slightly upward direction, then lift and release it in a perpendicular manner without spraying it. This is to avoid overextending the end of the line and keep it slightly blunt.

* The resulting 'ㄱ' is tilted in shape.

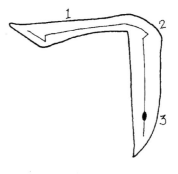

ㄱ (고 교 bottom consonant)

1. Start the horizontal line in the same way as the vowel 'ㅡ'. Move the stroke further by lifting the brush tip to thin out the resulting segment until it is properly lengthened.

2. Press the brush tip horizontally in a slightly downward direction. Without slowing speed, raise the brush hairs and move the brush tip down straight. Doing this helps avoid creating an unnecessarily prominent node and results in a sharply bent corner, a key characteristic of this mode of 'ㄱ'.

3. Nearing the end, pause the brush tip momentarily, draw the brush hairs together, and lift and release the brush tip.

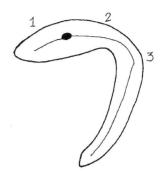

ㄱ (구 규 그)

1. Place the brush tip on paper to the right in a rolled over fashion and keep pressing it briefly. This results in a horizontal starting head tilted in a slightly upward direction.

2. Lift the brush tip, turn and move it briefly to the right in a slightly downward curve.

3. Raise the brush hairs, adjust the direction of the brush tip leftwards and move it downward and only slightly to the left. Finish the resulting diagonal segment as described.

* Unlike 'ㄱ' of '가', the resulting 'ㄱ' is not tilted.

ㅋ (카 캬 키 켜 키 코 쿄 bottom consonant 쿠 큐 크)

'ㅋ' can be written the same way as 'ㄱ' except that an additional horizontal line is added in the middle of 'ㄱ'. This second *hoek*, central stroke, is made in the same way as 'ㅡ' but much shorter and weaker than the vowel. Press the brush tip only lightly at its terminal end so that it does not stand out.

쿠 큐 크

코 쿄 bottom consonant

카 캬 키 켜 키

ㄴ (나 냐 니)

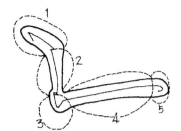

1. Place the brush tip at a substantially tilted angle as shown. Make the starting head similar to (as pronounced as) that of the vowel 'ㅣ'.

2. Raise the brush hairs, lift the brush tip slightly, and move it in a short vertical stroke.

3. Adjust the brush hairs upright and pause the brush tip. This creates a node from which the horizontal line is started.

4. Raise the brush hairs and move the brush tip horizontally to the right in a slightly upward direction. The resulting segment should be sufficiently long to connect with a vowel afterwards.

5. Lightly press the brush tip at the end, pause and release it.

ㄴ (너 녀)

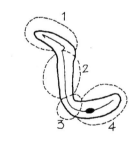

1. 1 and 2 are carried out as described.

3. Without making a node, turn the brush tip counterclockwise to make a round corner.

4. As soon as 3 is done, press the brush tip to the right in a slightly upward direction. Then lift the brush tip and keep moving it for a moment until pausing and releasing it. The horizontal segment is approximately as half long as that of 'ㄴ' of '나'. The top edge of this segment should appear straight whereas the bottom arches slightly.

* In '너', the horizontal interval space occupied by 'ㄴ' and that by 'ㅓ' should be equal.

ㄴ (ㅗ ㅛ ㅜ ㅠ ㅡ)

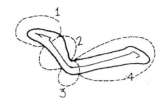

1. Place the brush tip nearly horizontally and make a starting head not as large as that of 'ㄴ' of 'ㅓ' or 'ㅕ'.

2. Move the brush tip down and in a rightward direction.

3. Turn the brush tip counterclockwise and adjust its direction to the right so that the ensuing horizontal line can be started. This movement tends to create a node, but keep it barely standing out.

4. Make a horizontal line. When complete, press the brush tip slightly downward, thereby rounding the terminal end. Pause and release the brush tip.

* The length of the resulting horizontal segment should be shorter than that of a vowel to be written underneath. Specifically, 'ㄴ' should be placed inside of two imaginary vertical lines that intersect the inner ends of the starting head and the terminal end of the vowel 'ㅡ'.

ㄴ (bottom consonant)

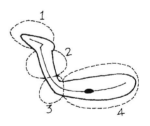

1. To make a starting head, lightly place the brush tip nearly horizontally and press it to the right in a bouncing manner so that it can be lifted immediately afterwards. This makes the resulting head less pronounced.

2. Lift the brush tip slightly and move it in a short vertical stroke in a slightly rightward direction.

3. Turn the brush tip counterclockwise to make a round corner without creating a node.

4. Press the brush tip to the right horizontally. Then lift the brush tip and move it in a slightly upward direction until adequate length is attained. Pause for a moment and release the brush tip. The resulting horizontal segment resembles that of 'ㄴ' of 'ㅓ' but should be substantially longer than that.

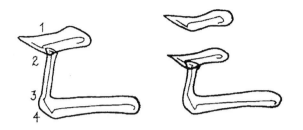

'ㄷ' is composed of a short horizontal line (first *hoek*) combined with 'ㄴ' underneath (second *hoek*). Hence, it can be written as such. Since the 'ㄴ' section begins within the top horizontal line, however, the brush tip touches and is kept pressed in a narrower fashion than in the case of 'ㄴ'. This thins the vertical segment that follows. (The vertical stroke can even lean slightly to the left.) These features make the 'ㄴ' section of 'ㄷ' shaped differently from 'ㄴ'.

| 받침 | 도됴두듀드 | 더뎌 | 다댜디 |

ㄷ ㅌ (다 댜 디)

1. Make the top line straight in a slightly more upward direction than a standard horizontal line.
2. Place the brush tip in a bouncing manner in the inside of the line where the starting head of the top line ends. Raise the brush hairs.
3. Move the brush down, resulting in a vertical stroke in a slightly leftward direction.
4. Lift the brush tip upright and press it downward to the right, creating a node. Use the returning lift from the node to make a horizontal line to the right. When complete, stop by pressing the brush tip slightly and then release it. The resulting horizontal segment should be approximately twice as long as the top horizontal line (excluding the protruding head length).

ㄷ (더 뎌 도 됴 두 듀 드 bottom consonant)

1. For 'ㄷ' of '더', make the first *hoek* (top horizontal stroke) as described with 'ㄷ' of '다'.
2. Likewise, start the second *hoek* from within the first *hoek*, and move the brush down.
3. Make a round corner and horizontal stroke as described with 'ㄴ' of '너' (p. 13). The terminal end of the resulting horizontal stroke should be aligned vertically with that of the top *hoek*.

* 'ㄷ' of '도' and 'ㄷ' as a bottom consonant can be written similarly to 'ㄴ' of '노' and a bottom 'ㄴ', respectively. In either case, the terminal ends of the first *hoek* (top stroke) and the second *hoek* (bottom stroke) should be aligned vertically.

ㄹ (라 랴 리 려 려 로 료 루 류 르 bottom consonant)

'ㄹ' is composed of 'ㄱ' combined with 'ㄷ' underneath. The horizontal stroke of 'ㄷ' directly supports 'ㄱ' (written as 'ㄱ' of 'ㅗ', p. 11). Hence, it can be written as such. However, if 'ㄹ' functions as an initial consonant, the upper 'ㄱ' section should not be weaker than the lower 'ㄷ' section. Conversely, when 'ㄹ' is an ending consonant, the lower 'ㄴ' section should not be weaker than the upper 'ㄱ' section.

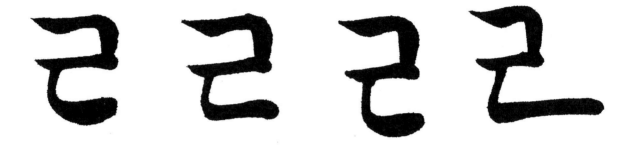

ㅌ (타 탸 티 텨 텨 토 툐 투 튜 트 bottom consonant)

'ㅌ' is composed of a horizontal line (first *hoek*) and a separate 'ㄷ' (second and third *hoek*s) underneath. Hence, it can be written as such. The top horizontal *hoek* should not be weaker than the second *hoek* (top horizontal stroke of 'ㄷ'). The spacing between the first and second *hoek*s and that between the second *hoek* and the bottom horizontal stroke should be equal.

ㅁ

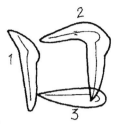

* 'ㅁ' is written in a single shape irrespective of combining vowels.

1. Place the brush tip gently and move it down to make a vertical line. This creates the first *hoek* at left.

2. Place the brush tip at the height of the midpoint of the starting head of the first *hoek* but slightly off to its right side. Make the top line segment of the second *hoek* as with the starting head of 'ㄱ' of 'ㄱ' (p. 12). Then without lifting the brush tip, turn it to a vertical direction. This helps maintain the thickness of the resulting bent corner and prevents a node from prominently standing out. Move the brush tip down. The resulting vertical stroke should be shorter than the previously made first *hoek* (1).

3. Place the brush tip lightly at the bottom edge of the first *hoek*. Press the brush tip and move it to the right horizontally. To finish the line, press the brush tip only slightly, lift and release it. The resulting third *hoek* (bottom stroke) connects with the vertical segment of the second *hoek*. Make certain that the bottom edge of the third *hoek* should not be placed lower than the bottom end of the first *hoek*.

* As a consequence, a fairly square quadrangle is created within the center of 'ㅁ'.

ㅂ

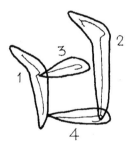

* 'ㅂ' is written in a single shape irrespective of combining vowels.

1. The first *hoek* (vertical line at left) is written the same way as 'ㅁ'.

2. Make the starting head of the second *hoek* (vertical line at right) by placing the brush tip at a higher position (the height of an additional starting head) and angled more horizontally than the first *hoek*'s starting head. Firmly press the brush tip and move it solidly down as with the vowel 'ㅣ'.

3. Lightly place the brush tip at the bottom edge of the head of the first *hoek*. Make a short horizontal stroke to the right by rolling the brush tip over slightly upward, similarly to the upper horizontal point of 'ㅕ' (p. 9). This creates the third *hoek*.

4. Make the fourth *hoek* (bottom horizontal line) as with 'ㅁ' (3).

* As with 'ㅁ', the resulting central quadrangle should appear fairly square.

ㅇ

* 'ㅇ' is written in a single shape irrespective of combining vowels.

Place the brush tip at the top of a prospective circle and move it to the right in a clockwise direction. Keep movement slow and steady. This generates outward force that will cause the brush tip to point towards its periphery and help create a smooth circle. Maintain the brush perpendicular while moving it so that the thickness of the resulting circle remains even.

ㅎ

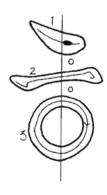

1. To make the first *hoek* (top point), place the brush tip lightly and press it diagonally to the right. Then lift the brush tip slightly, and pause and release it horizontally.

2. For the second *hoek* (central horizontal line), move the brush tip straight to the right in a slightly upward direction. The resulting line should be short.

3. Make 'ㅇ' under the second stroke so that its center is aligned vertically with the midpoint of the first *hoek*. Use the centrifugal pressure to create an undistorted circle.

* The spacing between the top point and the central horizontal line and that between the central horizontal line and 'ㅇ' should be equal.

ㅅ (사 샤 시)

* 'ㅅ' is not only a widely used consonant but also constitutes the backbone of 'ㅈ' and 'ㅊ'. Careful practice is recommended so as to be able to write its various forms correctly.

1. Place the brush tip at an angle as shown and make a long and straight head to the right and downward. As a result, the brush tip is brought to the lower center of the head.

2. Raise the brush hairs to perpendicular by moving them upwards. This will facilitate using the inner core of the brush tip to start the next diagonal line.

3. Move the brush diagonally to the left and downward. While moving, lift the brush gradually to make the stroke progressively thinner.

4. Adjust the brush tip horizontally, then lift and release it carefully leftwards. Do not spray the brush tip.

5. Add a point to the right corner of the diagonal line. Place the brush tip lightly at the edge of the line and press it diagonally down to the right. While moving, turn the brush tip further downward in a clockwise direction so that the resulting end is slightly bent.

ㅅ (사 샤 시)

ㅅ (서 셔)

The first *hoek* (head and diagonal stroke) is made as previously described. For the second *hoek* (point in the right corner), place the brush tip at the midpoint of the diagonal stroke and press it downward and to the right. Immediately afterwards, lift the brush tip, adjust its direction vertically, and move it down in a short line. While moving, lift the brush tip slightly to taper the bottom end so that the terminal half of the resulting vertical line does not appear heavier than its beginning half. Approaching the end of the line, pause and calmly release the brush tip without leaving a short pointed end. The length of the vertical *hoek* is slightly shorter than that of the straight segment of the upper diagonal line excluding its starting head.

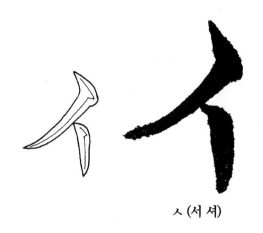

ㅅ (서 셔)

ㅅ (소 쇼 수 슈 스)

The top diagonal stroke is more horizontal and shorter in length than that of '사' or '서'. Its diagonal segment should be nearly the same length as its preceding head. For the point in the right corner, place the brush tip lightly at the edge of the starting head of the first *hoek*, then press it horizontally to the right. While moving, press the brush tip slightly downward to make the point curved, then pause and release it. The resulting 'ㅅ' appears strikingly fattened compared with that of '사' or '서'. When writing '수', '슈' or '스', the space between 'ㅅ' and the vowel below it should equal the height of the flattened 'ㅅ'.

ㅅ (소 쇼 수 슈 스)

ㅈ (자 쟈 지 저 져 조 죠 주 쥬 즈)

'ㅈ' is composed of a short top horizontal line supported by 'ㅅ' underneath. Started as with the vowel 'ㅡ', the top line is made by moving the brush tip straight to the right in a slightly upward direction, and ended by rounding the brush tip up. Afterwards, 'ㅅ' is added below by placing the brush tip where the starting head of the top line ends.

| 조죠주쥬즈 | 저 져 | 자 쟈 지 |

ㅊ (차 챠 치 처 쳐 초 쵸 추 츄 츠)

'ㅊ' is composed of a top point and a separate 'ㅈ' underneath. For the top point, press the brush tip diagonally to the right, adjust its direction horizontally as if slightly turning it counterclockwise, and then pause it momentarily and release it. Afterwards, add 'ㅈ' at bottom as described.

| 초쵸추츄츠 | 처 쳐 | 차 챠 치 |

ㅍ (퐈 퍄 픠)

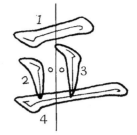

1. The first *hoek* (top horizontal line) is made as the top stroke of 'ㄷ' (p. 15).

2. The remaining points and lines are made similarly to 'ㅂ' (p. 17). The second *hoek* (left central vertical point) is made by delicately placing the brush tip, rolling the brush tip over slightly, adjusting its direction vertically, and moving it down.

3. The third *hoek* (right central vertical point) is made by placing the brush tip more horizontally and moving it straight down.

4. The fourth *hoek* (bottom horizontal line) is made as with the vowel 'ㅡ' except that its terminal end is made less pronounced by only slightly pressing the brush tip. The resulting stroke should be long enough to connect with a vowel to the right.

* Each of the two central vertical points (2 and 3) should be placed at equal distance from an imaginary vertical line coming from the midpoint of the top horizontal stroke.

ㅍ (퍼 펴)

The fourth *hoek* (bottom horizontal line) is almost as short as the top stroke. Its terminal end is made less pronounced by rounding the brush tip up.

ㅍ (포 표 푸 퓨 프 bottom consonant)

The space between the two central vertical points is significantly wider than that of '퐈' or '퍼'. This makes the resulting 'ㅍ' seem noticeably flatter. The horizontal line at bottom should be made with less of an upward slant so that the resulting fourth *hoek* has a stable horizontal shape.

명 새

랑 아

한 첨

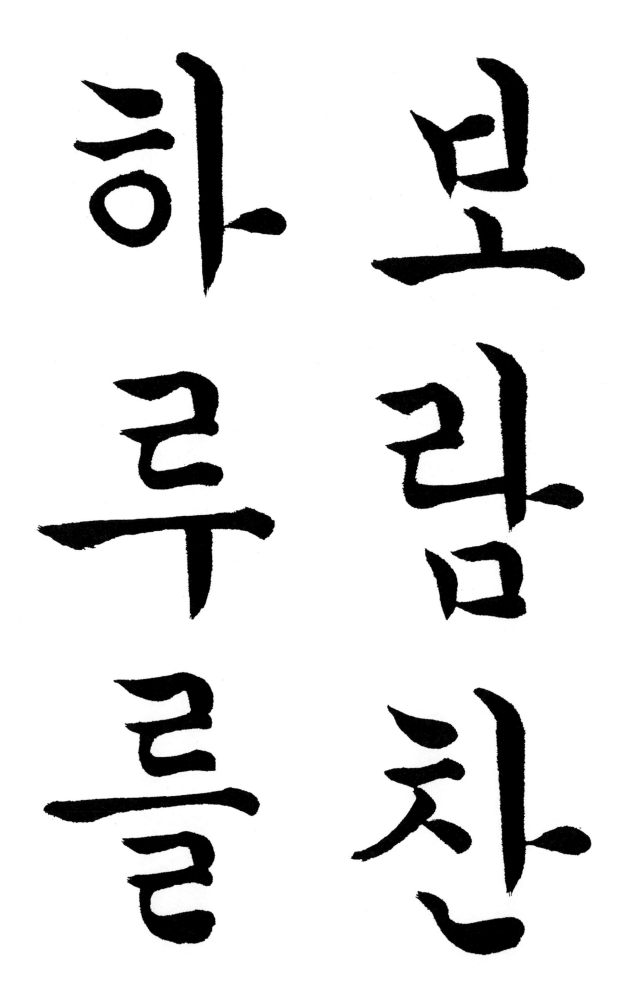

하 보
루 람
를 찬

대보름

달맞이

꽃놀이

널뛰기

등 끌째기
성이

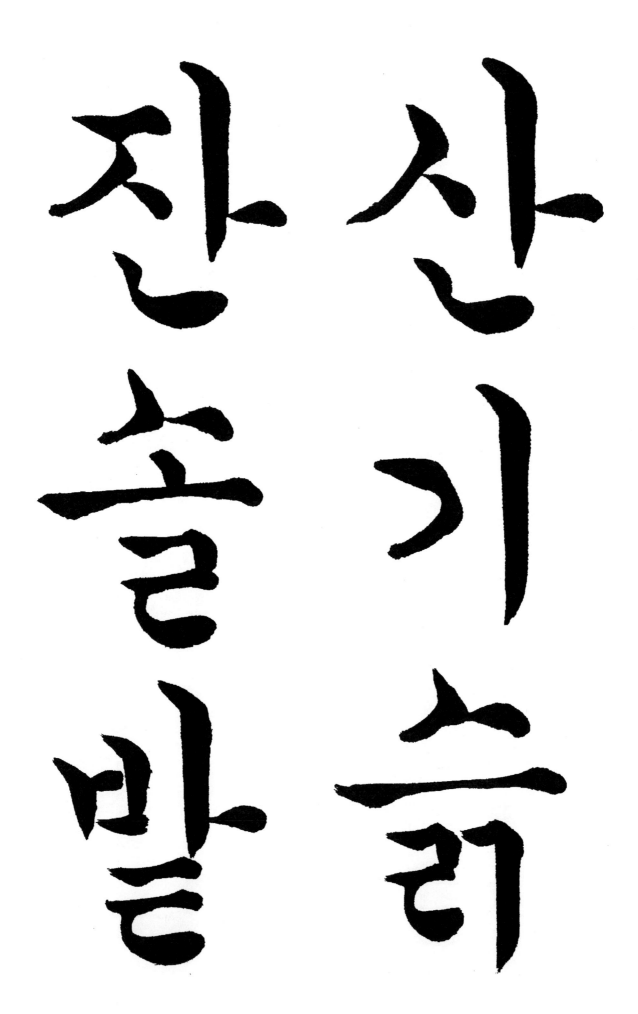

무등산

규봉암

제주도
백록담

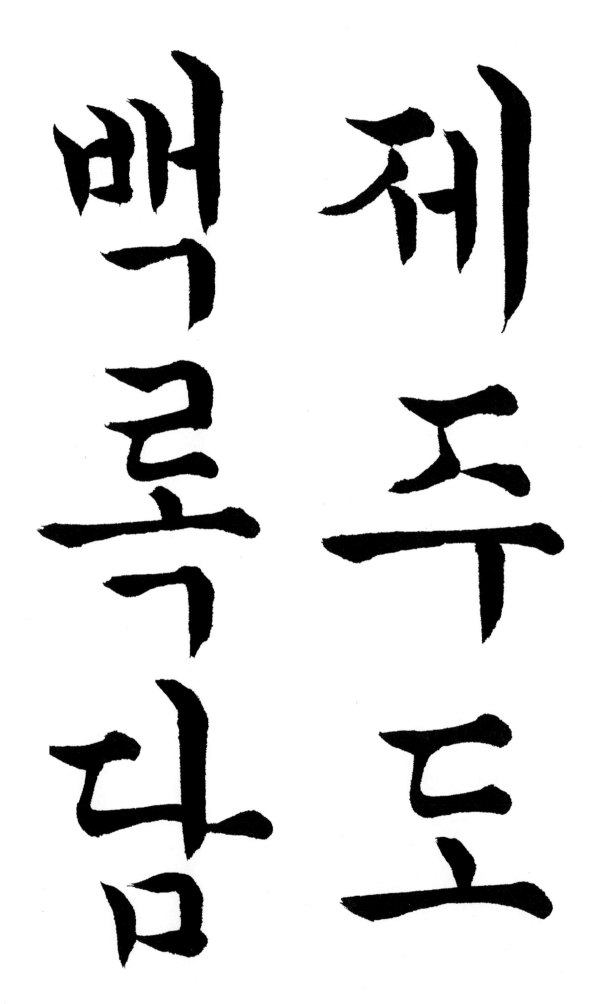

화선지

양호 붓

구운몽

춘향전

칼
비
쩜

다
려
뒤
김

즐거운 들놀이

세상에
빛되라

불우이

웃듬자

쇠
귀
에
경
읽
기

아 티

애 끌

산 모

고생 끝에

낙이 있다

지성이면

감천이라

협동정신

미풍양속

산이 있으면 골도 있다

삼일운동 민족자결

슬기로운 우리 겨레

하루 물림

열흘을 간다

천리 길도
한 걸음에

Writing double consonants

A double consonant is composed of two equal or different consonants that occupy a single top or bottom position in a given character. Hence, writing a double consonant requires compositional balance. To write a balanced double consonant, the first (left) consonant should not be larger than the second (right) one.

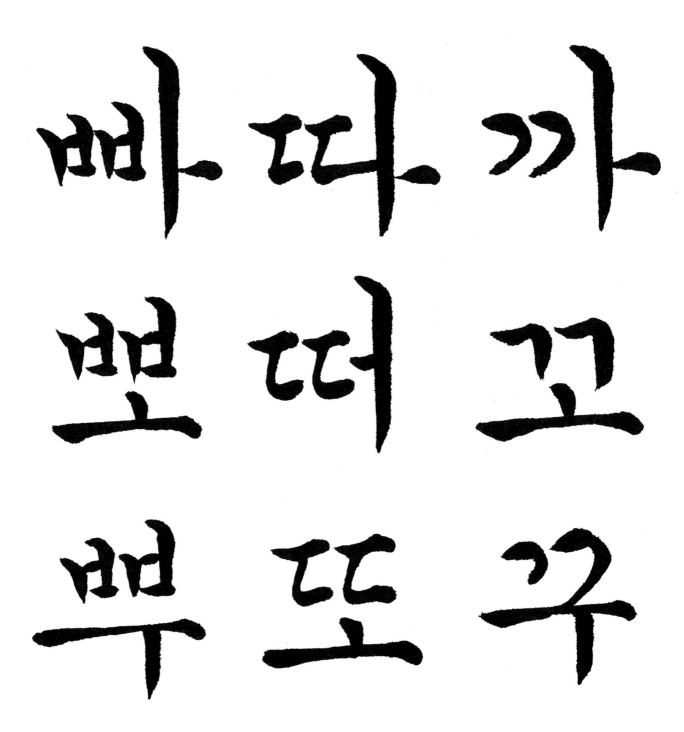

앉 밖 꽈

맍 볶 꿔

긇 넜 꺾

낢 못 뉘

겠 짜 싸

졌 쩌 써

있 쪼 쏘

했 쭈 쑤

을 밟 굴
릆 랩 리

할 짜 맑
랃 랩 리

뚜 듯 곪
릉 릿 릎

아 값 삵
릉 값 램

49

나는 듯 숨은

소리 못 듣는

다 없을 쏜가

다 려 돌

움 고 으

직 곳 려

이 곳 터

려 마 지

어 알 나

이 련 비

더 만 야

린 날 항

고 기 마

쳔품이 높은 젼차웃음에 도절조로다

구름 날고 섬 뜨고 하늘 푸른데 청옥빛 깊은 바다 산호당 속에

아름다운 비밀

이 숨어 있으

하얀 조개 꿈꾸

눈금 모랫가에

끝없이 밀려오는 물결 위로 나도 가고 배도 가고 바람도 간다

녹두밭에 앉지 마라 녹두꽃이 떨어지면 청포장수 울고 간다

Writing small characters

To manifest the characteristic beauty of small characters, fine and delicately made points and lines are essential. For this, additional care should be taken to make every single point and *hoek*.

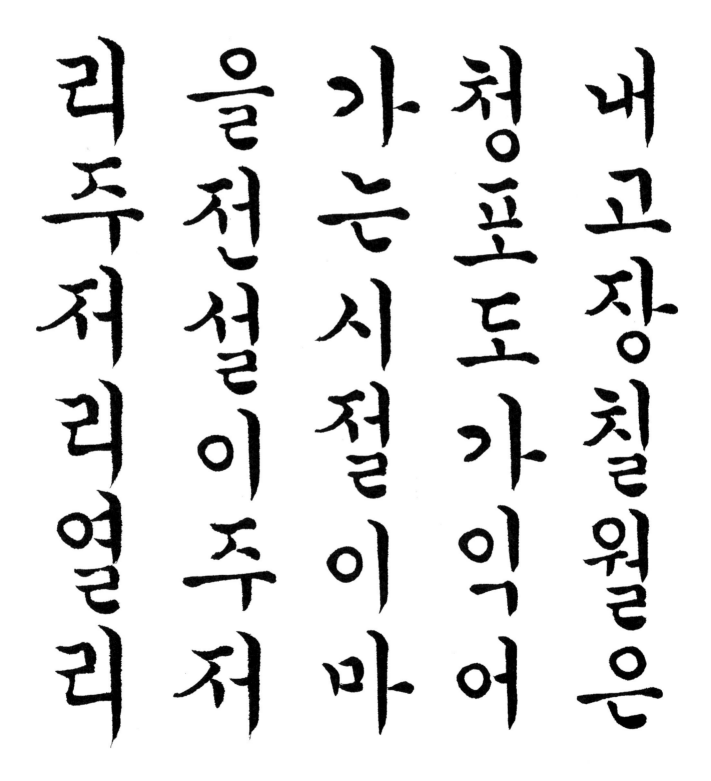

리주저리열리 을전설이주저 가는시절이마 청포도가익어 내고장칠월은

고 먼 데 하늘이 꿈꾸
며 알알이 들어와 박
혀 하늘 밀푸른 바다
가 가슴을 열고 흰 듯
단 배가 곱게 밀려서

오면

내가 바라는 손님은 고달픈 몸으로 청포를 입고 찾아온다고 했으니 내 그를 맞아 이 포도를 따 먹

으면 두 손을 함뿍 적셔도 좋으련

아이야 우리 식탁엔 은쟁반에

하이얀 모시 수건을 마련해 두렴

이육사

61

삭풍은나무끝에불고

명월은눈속에찬데만

리변성에일장검짚고

서서긴파람큰한소리

에거칠것이없에라

62

내 벗이 몇이나 하니 수석과 송죽이라

동산에 달 오르니 더욱 반갑고야

두어라 이 다섯 밖에 또 더하여 무엇하리

청산은어찌하여만고에프르르며유수난어찌하여주야에긋지아니난고우리도그치지말아만고상청하리라

입 다문 꽃봉오리 무슨 말씀 지니신고 피어나 빈 것일진대 다문 채로 겹소서

Once asked what seems to be the most important thing in calligraphy, Gotdeul answered that the quality of *hoek* – inadequately translated as brush stroke – is most critical. This is consistent with her words in 'About Calligraphy Writing' (p. 4) that learning how to do basic *hoek*s is of foremost importance. In other words, how *hoek*s are written is what calligraphy is all about. The Hangeul word '*hoek*' is used repeatedly in this book as the English word 'stroke' cannot adequately or fully express the soulful nature of *hoek*. Calligraphy is not about amusing drawings of strange Asian letters and characters on paper. It takes several years of intensive training and practice for professional calligraphy artists to master how to write every *hoek* correctly. The importance of practice cannot be overemphasized, as evidenced in Gotdeul's statement that calligraphy should be studied with one's arms, rather than the eyes. The free arm movement facilitated by a relaxed brush grip and upright posture is the key to successful brush handling, and this physical condition is only attained through incessant practice.

The Cursive Style

ㅏ (간 말)

*   Vowels in the cursive style are basically written the same way as the print style. However, because the cursive style often requires continuous movement due to its faster writing speed, differences exist in how to connect a vowel to a consonant and vice versa. Hence it is important that beginning learners do not attempt to write the cursive form rapidly. As in the print style, brush strokes should be carried out as slowly as possible.

1. For the horizontal point of 'ㅏ', place the brush tip to the right of the vowel at a distance roughly equal to the distance to the initial consonant to its left side and on an imaginary horizontal line crossing the bottom edge of the consonant. Press the brush tip horizontally to the right and downward, and lift it upright.

2. Move the brush tip straight to the left and downward toward the starting end of the ending consonant. The resulting thin line should connect the bottom end of the vowel 'ㅏ' to the consonant. From there, the cursive style for 'ㄴ' or 'ㄹ' can be carried out as described (see p. 79). As evident in this example, a thin connective line is an important general feature of the cursive style.

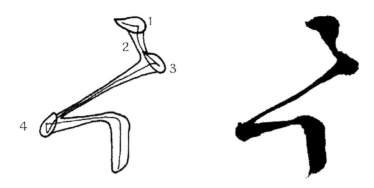

ㅑ (약 빰)

1. Place the brush tip slightly off to the right side of the vowel, approximately on an imaginary horizontal line crossing the top edge of the initial consonant. Press the brush tip to the right horizontally to make the first (top) horizontal point of 'ㅑ'. Lift the brush tip upright.

2. Move the brush tip down making a thin and vanishing connective vertical segment.

3. Press the brush tip to the right horizontally in a slightly downward direction. This results in the second (lower) horizontal point of 'ㅑ'. Lift the brush tip upright.

4. Continue to move the brush tip straight to the left and downward towards where the ending consonant is to be started. The resulting thin line thus passes through the bottom end of the vowel 'ㅑ', joining it to the consonant. From there, the cursive style for 'ㄱ' or 'ㅁ' can be carried out as described (see p. 82).

ㅓ (너 더 러)

* Two methods can be used to write 'ㅓ'.

1. The cursive 'ㅓ' can be written as in the print style. After completing the beginning consonant at left, release the brush tip and place it anew to make the horizontal point.

2. Alternatively, keep movement by completing the consonant and continuing to make the point. This creates a thin upward connective segment that joins the consonant to 'ㅓ'. Early calligraphers used the former method (1.) more frequently than the latter.

ㅓ (거 서 저)

1. At the terminal end of the initial consonant, stop for a moment and lift the brush nearly off the paper to make only a thin touching tip.

2. Move the brush tip to the right and upward, backward through the diagonal segment of the consonant.

3. When the brush tip exceeds the right edge of the consonant, adjust the brush tip horizontally in a slightly upward direction and continue movement. This creates the horizontal point of 'ㅓ', which is directly connected from the consonant at left. When the resulting point is long enough to be combined with 'ㅣ', pause and release the brush tip.

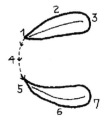 

ㅕ (셔 며 여 쳐 려 텨 펴)

1. For the upper horizontal point, place the brush tip lightly at the edge of the beginning consonant.

2. Press the brush tip to the right and upward and continue to move it horizontally. The resulting upper horizontal point is slightly arched upwards.

3. Pause, lift, and release the brush tip.

4. Move the brush backward as if returning through the stroke (upper horizontal point) just created. Continue to move the brush (hovering above the page) to the place from which to start the lower horizontal point.

5. Lightly place the brush tip at the lower edge of the consonant.

6. Press the brush tip to the right and downward and continue to move it horizontally.

7. Pause, lift, and release the brush tip. The resulting lower horizontal point is slightly arched downwards. The bottom edges of the consonant and the lower point should align horizontally with each other.

* For 'ㅕ' of '쳐', '려', '텨' and '펴', the upper horizontal point can be started directly from the beginning consonant by using a thin upward connective segment as described with '거' and '너' (p. 70).

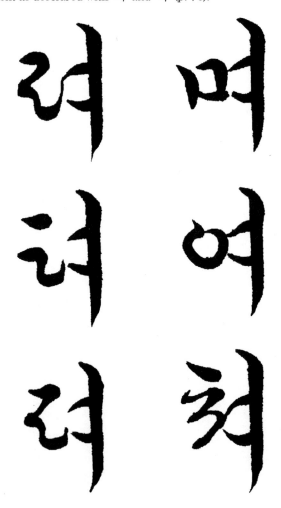

ㅗ (노 도 로 모 보 소)

* Write 'ㅗ' of 'ㅛ' and 'ㅋ' as in the print style (p. 11). In all the other combinations, 'ㅗ' is written by connecting the vertical point of 'ㅗ' with a top consonant.

1. Start the vertical point of 'ㅗ' from the right terminal end of the top consonant. Lift the brush tip slightly and move it to the left and downward. The resulting diagonal line comprises the vertical point.

2. Move the brush tip further to the left horizontally by lifting the tip of the brush (not fully off the page).

3. Place the brush tip at the beginning of the horizontal line, lift it upright, and press it lightly for the starting head. Raise the brush hairs.

4. Move the brush tip to the right to make the horizontal line.

5. To finish the horizontal line, press the brush tip to the right and downward as if letting it droop, then pause, lift, and release it. The terminal end should not be made too lengthy.

* The starting head of the horizontal line (3) is made less prominently. Make the terminal end (5) more pronounced than the starting end (3).

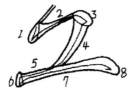 

ㅛ (요 죠 쇼 툐 표 효)

1. From the terminal end of the top consonant, lift the brush tip slightly, move it to the left and downward, and pause it momentarily. This results in the first node that is created in the same orientation as the direction of the movement. This node comprises the left vertical point of 'ㅛ'. Unlike in the print style, this point does not make contact with the bottom horizontal line.

2. Lift the brush tip and move it to the right in a slightly upward direction.

3. Finish the segment by lightly pressing the brush tip to the right and downward, creating the second node. This node comprises the right vertical point of 'ㅛ'.

4. From the second node, lift the brush tip slightly and move it to the left and downward. The resulting diagonal segment directly connects the right vertical point to the bottom horizontal line.

5. 5, 6, 7 and 8 are carried out as with 'ㅗ' (2 – 5) (p. 72).

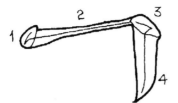 

ㅜ (구 누 두 루 무 부)

1. Make a thin connective line from the terminal end of the top consonant and place the brush tip at the beginning of the horizontal line. Delicate brushstroke makes the resulting connective line often invisible ('누', '두', '루', '무' and '부'). Press the brush tip to make the starting head. Because the movement direction of the thin connective line is kept, unlike a standard head of a horizontal *hoek* ('ㅡ'), this resulting head tilts in the opposite direction and isn't prominent. This illustrates another notable characteristic of the cursive style.

2. Raise the brush tip upright and move it straight to the right in a slightly upward slope. Thin out the resulting line by slightly lifting the brush tip through the movement. At the end, lift the brush tip almost completely.

3. Press the brush tip to the right horizontally to make a terminal node. Raise the brush hairs.

4. Adjust the brush tip and move it down vertically. The resulting vertical *hoek* should not be too long. Its length should be equal to ('구' and '누') or slightly shorter than ('두', '루', '무' and '부') the height of the top consonant including the gap space in between.

* The rightmost edge of 'ㅜ' should be aligned vertically with that of the top consonant.

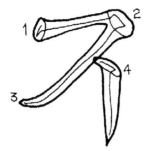 

ㅠ (슈 유 쥬 츄 퓨 휴)

1. The starting end is made by pressing the brush tip in the same direction as the connective line that follows from the terminal end of the top consonant. Lift the brush tip and make a horizontal line to the right. Because the beginning edge of the horizontal stroke matches more closely the leftmost edge of the top consonant, the resulting horizontal *hoek* becomes significantly shorter than that of 'ㅜ'.

2. Make the terminal node of the horizontal line as with 'ㅜ'. Then lift the brush tip, adjust its direction, and move it straight to the left and downward. This results in the first vertical stroke (left) of 'ㅠ', which will also be oriented diagonally.

3. To finish the diagonal line, pause and release the brush tip horizontally (in a similar manner to 'ㅅ', p. 19).

4. Place the brush tip at the edge of the first vertical line and press it to the right and downward. Lift the brush tip, adjust its direction, and move it down vertically. The resulting second vertical line can be tilted slightly to the right (as in the print style, p. 10). And its terminal end should be located lower than that of the first vertical line at left. The rightmost edge of the second vertical line should be aligned vertically with that of the top consonant.

ㄷ (다)

1. Make a horizontal point by pressing the brush tip as if rolling it over (similarly to 'ㄱ' of 'ㄱ', p. 12). Then lift the brush tip, turn it clockwise, and move it in a short downward stroke in a slightly leftward direction.

2. Press the brush tip vertically and slightly towards the right. This results in a node that serves as the starting end of the horizontal line. Raise the brush hairs upright, and move the brush to the right. The resulting horizontal line should be parallel to the top *hoek* and long enough to connect to 'ㅏ'.

* The cursive form of 'ㄷ' in '다' differs from the print form of 'ㄴ' in '나' (p. 13). The first stroke of the 'ㄷ' is long in an upward orientation whereas the head of the 'ㄴ' slants in a downward orientation.

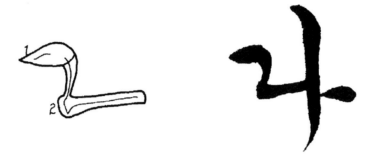

ㅌ (타)

1. Start the top horizontal line as in the print form of 'ㅌ' (p. 16) but end it in a much shortened way, virtually as a point.

2. 2 and 3 are carried out as with the cursive 'ㄷ' of '다'.

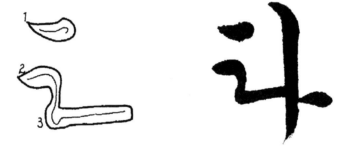

ㄹ (라)

1. The upper section of 'ㄹ' can be written as with 'ㄱ' of '가' (p. 11) in reduced size. At its terminal end, which is completed right below its starting head, lift the brush tip as if pushing it up slightly.

2. Press the brush tip downward, creating the first node. Combined with the previous move, this results in a fairly prominent node. Lift the brush tip and head to the right. Immediately afterwards, turn it clockwise in a short downward movement.

3. Press the brush tip vertically in a slightly rightward direction, creating the second node. Then adjust the brush tip upright, raise the brush hairs, and move the brush to the right to make a horizontal line.

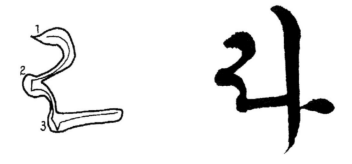

ㅍ (파)

1. Start the first *hoek* (top horizontal line) as if making a top horizontal point in the cursive 'ㅌ' of '타' (p. 76). Keep the resulting stroke straight and horizontal. From its terminal end, lift the brush tip and move it straight to the left and downward, resulting in a short diagonal segment. Taken together, this beginning section of 'ㅍ' is written with two successive linear strokes made in different directions whereas that of 'ㄹ' is made by a single continuous curving stroke. This is a key difference between the cursive 'ㅍ' and 'ㄹ'.

2. 2 and 3 are carried out as with the cursive 'ㄹ' (2 – 3, p. 76) except that the node (2) is made in the same orientation as the movement of the diagonal segment. Without lifting the brush tip up as much, the resulting first node of 'ㅍ' appears subtly different from the corresponding node of 'ㄹ'.

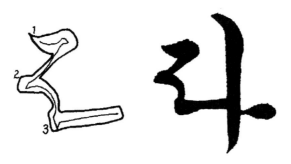

ㄷ ㅌ ㄹ ㅍ (더 타 러 펴)

* Make the upper section of these consonants identically to '다', '타', '라' or '파', respectively. For the lower section, omit the bottom node and a horizontal segment started from it. Instead, turn the brush tip counterclockwise, creating a round corner. Then, continue to turn the brush tip smoothly to form a round bottom in the stroke. Afterwards, lift the brush tip to thin out the connective line rising to the starting position of the horizontal point of 'ㅓ'.

ㄷ (됴)

1. Make the top horizontal line as in the print style (p. 15).

2. From the terminal end of the line, lift the pressed brush tip, then backtrack left through the line. Let the brush tip veer off before reaching where the starting head of the horizontal line ends.

3. Keep moving the brush tip to the left and downward. Adjust the brush tip vertically, and without pressing it, turn it counterclockwise, creating a round corner.

4. Continue to move the brush tip to the right horizontally in a relaxed manner, and pause, lift, and release it. This results in the bottom segment.

ㄹ (로)

'ㄹ' is composed of 'ㄱ' supported by 'ㄷ' underneath. Hence, the cursive 'ㄹ' as a top consonant is written accordingly. The upper 'ㄱ' section should be written as with 'ㄱ' of 'ㅗ' (p. 11).

ㅌ (토)

'ㅌ' is composed of a horizontal line and a separate 'ㄷ' underneath. Hence, the cursive 'ㅌ' as a top consonant is written accordingly. The top line and 'ㄷ' should be aligned vertically with each other.

ㅍ (표)

1. Make a short horizontal line.

2. From the terminal end of the line, lift the pressed brush tip, then move it straight to the left and downward. This results in a thin connective line.

3. Press the brush tip in the same direction as the connecting line movement, creating the first node. The resulting node comprises the left vertical point of 'ㅍ', which does not make contact with the bottom horizontal line. Lift the brush tip and move it lightly to the right and upward to make a thin horizontal connective stroke.

4. Press the brush tip to the right horizontally in a slightly downward direction, creating the second node. This node comprises the right vertical point of 'ㅍ'. Lift the brush tip and move it to the left and downward, resulting in a diagonal connective segment.

5. Lightly press the brush tip vertically to make the starting end of the bottom horizontal line. Move the brush tip to the right and complete the line.

* Brush skills used here (2 – 5) are essentially the same as those used for 'ㅛ' (1 – 5, p. 73).

ㄴ (른 bottom consonant)

1. From the terminal end of the vowel '—', lift the pressed brush tip, relax, and move it to the left and downward.

2. Finish the resulting diagonal connective line at a position not exceeding an imaginary vertical line that connects to the leftmost edge of the top consonant 'ㄹ'. Turn the brush tip counterclockwise without pressing it, resulting in a round corner.

3. Immediately afterwards, press the brush tip to the right and move it briefly. Then lift the brush tip, move it upward slightly, and pause and calmly release it.

ㄷ (듣 bottom consonant)

1. The top horizontal line is made as in the print style (p. 16). However, the beginning of this short stroke is connected with an almost invisible connective line originating from the terminal end of the above vowel '—'.

2. When the top line is complete, lift the pressed brush tip at its terminal end and move it to the left and downward. From the resulting connective segment, the rest is carried out as with the cursive bottom 'ㄴ'.

ㅌ (끝 bottom consonant)

'ㅌ' is composed of a top horizontal line and a separate 'ㄷ' underneath. Hence, the cursive 'ㅌ' as a bottom consonant is written accordingly. The top line should not be shorter than the width of the lower 'ㄷ'.

ㄹ (늘 bottom consonant)

1. From the terminal end of the vowel '—', move the brush tip to the left and downward. This results in a thin connective line that ends at the beginning of 'ㄹ'. Following the direction of the connective stroke, press the brush tip to create the first node (the starting end of 'ㄹ'). Then lift the brush tip and move it to the right.

2. Pause the brush tip, press it to the right horizontally. This creates the second node. Lift the brush tip and again move it to the left and downward.

3. Finish the resulting segment at a position slightly rightward of the first node. Pause the brush tip to create the third node. Adjust the brush tip slightly upward and begin a short movement to the right, back through the previously made left and downward segment. Let the brush tip veer out soon after and continue to move it horizontally slightly further.

4. Press the brush tip to the right horizontally, creating the fourth node. Lift the brush tip and move it to the left and downward again.

5. When this resulting connective line reaches a position slightly rightward of the third node, turn the brush tip counterclockwise. This results in a round corner.

6. The horizontal bottom segment is made as with the cursive bottom 'ㄴ'. Overall, the process described above helps to progressively thin out 'ㄹ' downwardly on its left side.

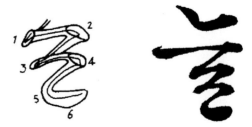

ㅈ (자)

1. The top horizontal line is made as in the print style (p. 20). Unlike the print style, however, movement continues for the next diagonal line.

2. From the terminal end of the horizontal line, raise the pressed brush tip upright, and move it straight to the left and downward.

3. Finish the resulting diagonal line by adjusting the brush tip horizontally and lifting and releasing it calmly to the left.

4. The point in the right corner is made as in the print style.

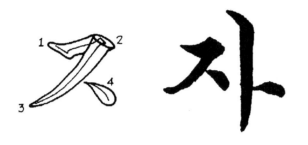

ㅊ (차)

1. The top point is made as in the print style (p. 20). Press the brush tip in a bouncing manner, lift it nearly completely, and move it to the beginning of the horizontal line.

2. Place the brush tip vertically as if keeping the direction of an invisible connective line, and press it slightly, making the starting head of the horizontal line. The resulting starting head is much less prominent than in the print style. Lift the brush tip upright, relax, and move it to the right.

3. 3, 4 and 5 are carried out as with the cursive 'ㅈ' (2 – 4).

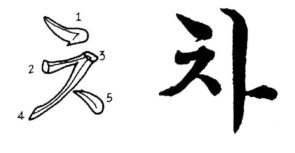

ㅅ (서)

1. Place and firmly press the brush tip in a downward and slightly rightward direction. This creates a starting head as prominent as 'ㅅ' of '서' in the print style (p. 19). Lift the brush tip upright and move it to the left and downward. The resulting diagonal segment should be as short as the starting head.

2. At the terminal end of the diagonal segment, pause and slightly press the brush tip as if pushing it back upwards. Lift the brush tip and backtrack, moving right through the diagonal stroke.

3. Let the brush tip diverge before reaching the terminal end of the starting head, keep moving it briefly and lightly press it horizontally, creating a weak node. Immediately afterwards, adjust the brush tip and move it to the left and downward again, parallel to the first diagonal segment.

4. Finish the resulting second diagonal segment at a position rightward to the terminal end of the first diagonal segment so that its end is aligned vertically with the bottom center of the starting head. The rest is carried out as described (2). When the brush tip veers out, continue to move it to the right horizontally. At the end, the resulting horizontal line should be sufficiently long as it also becomes the horizontal point of the vowel 'ㅓ'.

ㅈ (저)

1. 1 and 2 are carried out as with the cursive 'ㅈ' of '자' except that the first diagonal line (2 – 3) is significantly shortened. Its terminal end should not exceed the starting head of the top horizontal line.

3. 3, 4 and 5 are carried out as with the cursive 'ㅅ' of '서' (2 – 4).

ㅊ (쳐)

1. 1, 2 and 3 are carried out as with the cursive 'ㅊ' of '차' (p. 80) except that the first diagonal line (3 – 4) is significantly shortened. Its terminal end should not exceed the starting head of the upper horizontal line.

4. 4, 5 and 6 are carried out as with the cursive 'ㅈ' of '저' (3 – 5, p. 80).

ㅈ (조)

'ㅈ' is written as with 'ㅈ' of '저' (p. 80) except that the lower section is made similarly to the cursive 'ㅅ' of '소'. As a result, the cursive 'ㅈ' of '조' is flattened and widened.

ㅊ (초)

'ㅊ' is written as with 'ㅊ' of '쳐' except that the lower section is made similarly to the cursive 'ㅈ' of '조'. As a result, the cursive 'ㅊ' of '초' is flattened and widened.

ㅅ (소)

1. Make a prominent starting head by pressing the brush tip downward in a slightly rightward direction. Lift the brush tip upright and move it to the left and downward, making a diagonal segment. The resulting stroke should be as short as the starting head. Pause the brush.

2. Lift the brush tip and backtrack to the right, tracing back through the previously made diagonal segment. Let the brush tip diverge before reaching the terminal end of the starting head, and keep moving it further horizontally.

3. Firmly press the brush tip to the right in a slightly downward direction as if letting it droop. This creates a fairly big node, which is the terminal end of the right point of 'ㅅ'. Keeping the brush tip connected, move it to the left and downward. The resulting diagonal line, to be connected to the bottom horizontal line, comprises the vertical point of 'ㅗ'.

* The overall shape of the resulting 'ㅅ' of '소' is significantly flat and wide.

ㅁ (무)

1. The first *hoek* (left vertical line) is made as in the print style (p. 17).

2. For the second *hoek*, place the brush tip slightly off to the right side of the starting head of the first *hoek*. Firmly press the brush tip horizontally to the right, creating the first node. Then lift the brush tip, adjust its direction vertically, and move it down.

3. Press the brush tip horizontally again as if making a point to the right and in a slightly downward direction. This creates the second node. Immediately afterwards, lift the brush tip, move it slightly to the left, then lift and release it in the same direction. This results in a short brush stroke thinning out to the left, a hallmark of the cursive 'ㅁ'. This thin stroke comprises the bottom horizontal line of 'ㅁ' and is often connected to the vowel underneath as with '무'.

*   Unlike in the print style, the three (top horizontal, right vertical, and bottom horizontal) segments of the cursive 'ㅁ' are made continuously with the brush in a single stroke.

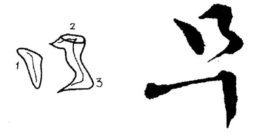

ㅁ (좀)

1. From the terminal end of the vowel above, lift the brush tip and move it to the left and downward. End the resulting thin connective line where the first *hoek* of 'ㅁ' is started. Pause the brush tip briefly. Without making a head, press the brush tip as if rolling it over and move it downward slightly towards the right. Pause the brush tip briefly. This creates the first node at the bottom. Lift the brush tip again, and move it upwards and to the right. The resulting thin segment comprises the top line segment of 'ㅁ'.

2. Press the brush tip horizontally to the right, creating the second node.

3. The rest is carried out as described for the cursive head 'ㅁ' (2 – 3).

*   All the lines and segments of the cursive bottom 'ㅁ' are made in a single stroke.

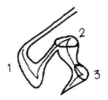

ㅅ (짓)

1. From the terminal end of the vowel ' ㅣ ', lift the brush tip and move it to the left and downward. The resulting thin connective line leads directly to the top diagonal line of 'ㅅ'. While moving, press the brush tip with increasing firmness to make the resulting lower part of the line gradually thicker. Keep the upper edge of the line even while letting the lower edge assume the role of varying in width. Note that in this process the starting head of 'ㅅ' is omitted.

2. Approaching the end of the diagonal line, slowly press the brush tip by adjusting it horizontally, and lift and release it to the left. This often results in a spectacularly extended end, a hallmark of the cursive bottom 'ㅅ'.

3. The point to the right is made as in the print style (p. 19).

ㅆ (졌)

1. Lift and move the brush tip to the left and downward from the terminal end of 'ㅕ'. The resulting thin connective line leads directly to the first bottom 'ㅅ' at left. Since two 'ㅅ's have to be accommodated, the thin connective line should extend significantly further towards the left than in the case of a single consonant, and consequently, is slightly bent.

2. The point in the right corner of the first 'ㅅ' (left) is made as in the print style except that it should be short so that the second 'ㅅ' (right) can be placed adequately.

3. The second 'ㅅ' (right) is written as in the print style.

4. The diagonal lines of the two 'ㅅ' letters should be parallel to each other. The two points in the right corner are placed evenly, too, under a single imaginary horizontal line that crosses their upper edges.

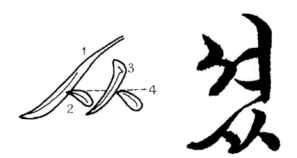

ㅇ (이)

1. The cursive 'ㅇ' is written differently from the print form. First, make a thin and straight vertical head in a slightly rightward direction. Lift the brush tip.

2. Turn the brush tip in the counterclockwise direction. As the brush tip passes the bottom of the resulting left half of the circle, lift and release the tip off the paper while leaving a thinning brush mark in the path to be taken by the right half of the circle. This is to enable the end of the left half circle to join and be covered by the ensuing right half circle so the full circle can be completed intact. Move the brush tip to the previously made vertical head to start the right half circle.

3. Gently place the brush tip horizontally, moving it in the clockwise direction. As the resulting right half circle reaches the brush mark of the left half circle, lift the brush tip slightly so that the two ends meet seamlessly. Release the brush tip when it completes the bottom of the resulting 'ㅇ'.

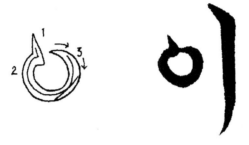

ㅇ (용)

1. From the terminal end of the vowel 'ㅛ', move the brush tip to the left and downward. The resulting connective line directly connects to the bottom 'ㅇ'. (A head is omitted.) Press the brush tip and circle it counterclockwise. Make the circumference of the resulting left half circle sufficiently thick. Pause and release the brush tip when it passes the bottom of the half circle. Leave brush mark in the path to be taken by the right half circle.

2. To make the right half circle, move and place the brush tip to a central position beneath the diagonal connective line. Start the right half circle by circling the brush tip in the clockwise direction. Let the ends of the two half circles meet seamlessly.

* Along an imaginary vertical line bisecting the center of the resulting character '용', the left and right halves of the character should be evenly distributed and balanced in weight to each other.

ㅎ (하)

1. The top point is made as in the print style (p. 18).

2. Make the central horizontal line straight and not too thick. The starting head of the horizontal line can be made as if connected to the top point.

3. From the terminal end of the horizontal line, lift the pressed brush tip and move it to the left and downward. The resulting short connective line directly connects to the left half circle of the bottom 'ㅇ'.

4. The right half circle can also be made as described with the cursive bottom 'ㅇ' (p. 84).

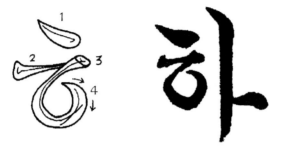

ㅂ (급)

From the terminal end of the vowel 'ㅡ', lift and move the brush tip to the left and downward. The resulting thin connective line connects to the bottom 'ㅂ'. Press the brush tip and delicately move it down, resulting in the left vertical line of 'ㅂ'. In the process, the starting head of the left vertical *hoek* is omitted. The rest is made as described in the print style (p. 17).

아름나

얼궁체

메 느

아 례

리 의

옥에

위잇

도

나

힘이라 별결은

물 붓기

걸

늘

에

이 백

붉 먹

기 고

봄

불

따

뜻

한

날

씨

울음
우리

찌그레
꽃

낯께

청꽃

해이

늘흥

호나

룩묵

붉은

쿵

싫은

힐든

장미꽃

국련회

덕악별

글바의

끝없는

수평선

래앙을뜨

너시뜰나

보
늘
삭
는

생
르
슬
이
라

삼

시

크

살

드

찍

글

항

브

체

즉장망혜

낭표자로

솟아나는 샘물처럼

길은실숙

뼈극즈리

호 록 장 옷

만 믈 치 마

푸른 하늘
흰구름 떼

넓은들판

황금물결

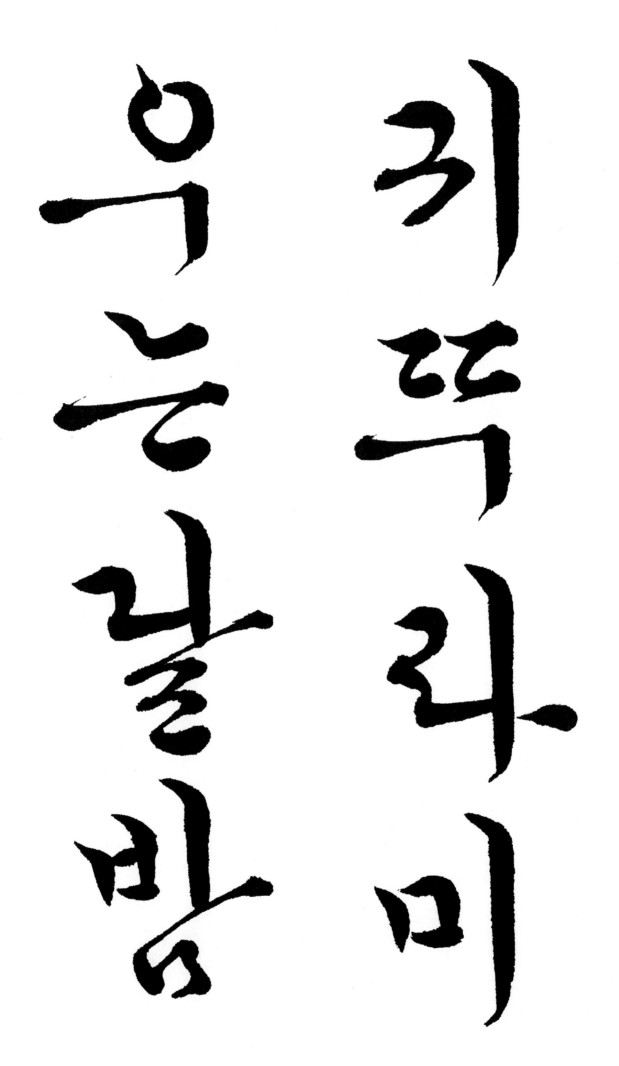

발없는말
천리간다

한슬밤에

배부를까

지
왕
제

리
봉
오

산
울
룰

쳥
언
꼬

청
학
동
집

어
둘
어
길

올
헤
밀
제

정 럭 칠

도 으 믈

하 리 압

라 라 욱

르　측　산

는　기　차

국　리　에

나　북　숙

리 쩍 낡

의 이 혜

바 는 는

라 능 편

도 쳐 츙

힌 하 윽

신 덩 공

도 을 맹

랑 아 동

창 호 짓

새 레 늘

벅 바 열

활
철
이
라

민
죽
의
박

오
눌
은
이

사공이 많으면 배가 산으로 올라간다

늘 방 바
른 아 쁘
이 에 게
있 도 찡
라 손 는

될 청 부 른 나

뚝 눈 떡 일 부

러 알 아 볼 가

야 이 구

보 라 슬

배 도 이

나 쩨 저

라 어 말

공 일 빛

하 새 나

이 뢰 는

안 릴 뢰

꽃 대 릴

꽃 동 꽃

아 글 마

놓 욱 나

은 비 동

돗 녀 글

또 라 이

한 우 아

옥 라 니

잠 이 아

회 름 름

돌 샘 돗

바 아 먹

락 돌 축

맑 옥 어

온 는 라

127

진흙

발

구

정

물

에

행

여

듬

울

나

칠

세

라

차
리
리
막
힐

지
언
정
흐
려

훌
러
가
리
오

산 너 머 남 촌 에

늣 누 가 실 길 래

해 마 다 봄 바 람

이 남 으 로 오 네

130

면 밀 면 꽃
보 익 진 픠
리 눈 늘 눈
내 오 래 사
웅 월 향 월
새 이 기 이

굼 엔 버 엔

잔 호 둘 중

거 랑 밭 날

넓 나 실 새

은 비 개 노

벌 때 쳥 래

어느 것 한 가지

들 실 어 인 오 리

남 출 서 남 름 물

제 나 는 좋 데 나

133

여럿이 가는데

섞이면 떠들다가

리도 굴려 간다

그 동과 질서와 청실이 있는 곳에 기쁨도 있다

내 죽으면 한 개 바

위가 되리라 아예

애련에 물들지 않

고 희로에 움직이

지
않
고
비
외
바
람

에
깎
이
는
데
로
억

녘
비
정
의
힘
둑
에

안
으
로
안
으
로
민

처찍질하여드러
어생명도망각하
고흐르는구름머
언원뢰끔끅어도

그래하지 않고 두
쪽으로 깨뜨려져
도 흔들리하지 않는
바위가 되리라

삿갓에 도롱이 입고 세
우중에 호미 메고 산 전
을흘 매다가 녹음에 누
웠으니 목동이 우양을
몰아 잠들 나를 깨와다

쌀나믈레올믈이고기

도곰맛이이체욕즘

울즐이괴더욱새변이

라나만깅님그릭잇으

로시람계위하고라

흰구름뭉뭉떠는골골
이잠겼는데추상에글
든남등꽃도곤더중아
라쳔공이나를위하여
떡빛을그며내도나

142

두렷신앙같수룰예듯

고이께보니도회뜬밝

은믈에심영조차짐졌

어라아희야우릉이어

니오나는예가하느라

어졔 녀ᄉ셔 셔

건군의 덕과 음양의 되 큰디라 ᄡ 건은아 비

라 일로ᄭ고 은어 미 라 일로ᄭ나 하니 과 사름이

곳ᄋ리라 일로 음양이 골오ᄒ여야 만믈이

화ᄒ고 무 뷔 화ᄒ여야 가 되이니 그런고로 그

라 희다 슬며 다스디 못ᄒ미 이 쏘ᄒ 져의 가속

ᄒ며 가ᄉ디 못ᄒ매 인ᄂ 라쥬여에 ㄹ오디무

뷔 이 신연ᄒ우에 무 지 잇고 부 지이 신연ᄒ우 군신이

잇다ᄒ고 무 진 쏘로 오샤 디 쏘치 부부에 진니다ᄒ

시고서 젼 삼빅 편의 군문은 곳이 남이 며 쥬문

Classic work by an old master / The print style / From "Womens' four books"

Classic work by an old master / The half cursive style / From "The list of bedclothes prepared for a princess' wedding"

Another important aspect of Gotdeul's calligraphy is informed by her education in music. Gotdeul graduated from the Department of Music at Ewha College, where she received intensive piano instruction from Mrs. Kathleen Gorman, a professor from England. The lessons took place in an atmosphere that respected each student's personality and the level of learning was so deep and sophisticated that one of her classmates later became a renowned pianist in Korea. Ironically, this instruction in western music provided an indispensable artistic foundation for her devotion to lifelong research in Hangeul calligraphy. As evidenced in the instructions and examples of this book, the cursive style often involves a ceaseless flow of brushwork comprised of multiple pauses and restarts of strokes in a continuous movement of the brush. This relaxed brushwork – frequently interrupted by pauses at accent-making nodes and the redirecting of strokes – comprises a rhythmic movement, and the brushwork as a whole then seems to become a musical performance. Therefore, finetuning this natural flow of rhythmic brushwork is key to successful cursive writing. Gotdeul once recalled that without this early education in classical music, it would have been difficult for her to dedicate herself to the study and instruction of Hangeul calligraphy throughout her life.

Appendix

Romanization of Hangeul Alphabets

Vowels (basic)		Romanization
ㅏ	아 [a]	a
ㅑ	야 [ja]	ya
ㅓ	어 [ɜ]	eo
ㅕ	여 [jɜ]	yeo
ㅗ	오 [o]	o
ㅛ	요 [jo]	yo
ㅜ	우 [u]	u
ㅠ	유 [ju]	yu
ㅡ	으 [ɤ]	eu
ㅣ	이 [i]	i

Vowels (composite)		Romanization
ㅐ	애 [æ]	ae
ㅒ	얘 [jæ]	yae
ㅔ	에 [e]	e
ㅖ	예 [je]	ye
ㅘ	와 [wa]	wa
ㅚ	외 [œ]	oe
ㅙ	왜 [wæ]	wae
ㅝ	워 [wɜ]	wo
ㅞ	웨 [we]	we
ㅟ	위 [wi]	wi
ㅢ	의 [ɤi]	ui

Consonants (basic)		Romanization
ㄱ	기역 [gijɜk]	g, k
ㄴ	니은 [niɤn]	n
ㄷ	디귿 [digɤt]	d, t
ㄹ	리을 [riɤl]	r, l
ㅁ	미음 [miɤm]	m
ㅂ	비읍 [biɤp]	b, p
ㅅ	시옷 [siot]	s
ㅇ	이응 [iɤng]	ng
ㅈ	지읒 [jiɤt]	j
ㅊ	치읓 [tʃiɤt]	ch
ㅋ	키읔 [kiɤk]	k
ㅌ	티읕 [tiɤt]	t
ㅍ	피읖 [piɤp]	p
ㅎ	히읗 [hiɤt]	h

Consonants (composite)		Romanization
ㄲ	쌍기역 [ssanggijɜk]	kk
ㄸ	쌍디귿 [ssangdigɤt]	tt
ㅃ	쌍비읍 [ssangbiɤp]	pp
ㅆ	쌍시옷 [ssangsiot]	ss
ㅉ	쌍지읒 [ssangjiɤt]	jj

Illustration of Tools for Hangeul Calligraphy

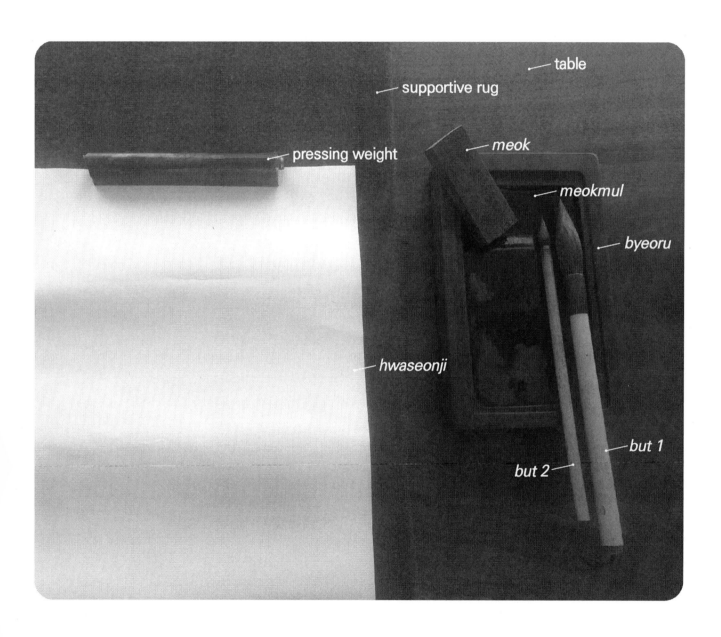

Translation of Calligraphic Examples

Pages 22 –

The print style: six characters

Pages 22 – 23

명랑한 새 아침
a lively new morning
보람찬 하루를
a rewarding day

Pages 24 – 25

대보름 달맞이
greeting the first full moon of the year
윷놀이 널뛰기
playing *yut* (traditional Korean game) and jumping *neol* (traditional Korean see-saw)

Pages 26 – 27

골짜기 등성이
valley and mountain ridge
산기슭 잔솔밭
small pine field at the bottom of a mountain

Pages 28 – 29

무등산 규봉암
Gyubongam of Mudeung Mountain
제주도 백록담
Baekrokdam of Jeju Island

Pages 30 – 31

화선지 양호붓
calligraphy paper and good brush
춘향전 구운몽
Chunhyangjeon and Gueunmong (old classic Hangeul novels)

Pages 32 – 33

갈비찜 닭튀김
steamed rib-eye and fried chicken
즐거운 들놀이
cheerful field excursion

Pages 34 – 35

세상에 빛 되라
Be the light of the world.
불우 이웃 돕자
Let's help poor neighbors.

Pages 36 – 37

쇠 귀에 경 읽기
reading scripture to a cow's ears
티끌 모아 태산
Gather the dust and make a mountain.

Pages 38 –

The print style: eight characters

Pages 38 – 39

고생 끝에 낙이 있다
Joy comes after hardship.
지성이면 감천이다
Sincerity moves heaven.

Pages 40 – 41

협동정신 미풍양속
collaborative spirit, virtuous atmosphere and good custom
산 있으면 골도 있다
If there is a mountain, there is a valley, too.

Pages 42 – 43

삼일운동 민족자결
The March 1st Independence Movement and national self-determination
슬기로운 우리 겨레
our wise people

Pages 44 – 45

하루 물림 열흘 간다
A day delayed cannot be caught up in ten days.
천리 길도 한 걸음에
A single first step makes a thousand miles.

Pages 50 –

The print style: fifteen characters

Pages 50 – 52

나는 듯 숨은 소리 못 듣는다 없을 쏜가
돋으려 터지려고 곳곳마다 움직이리
나비야 하마 알련만 날기 어이 더딘고
How could barely audible sound mean its absence?
Budding and blooming movement everywhere.
Butterflies might know it, but why does it take them so long to fly?
* From "Jochun" (Early spring), a *sijo* by Widang Jeong In-Bo (1893 – 1950)

Page 53

천품이 높은 전차 웃음에도 절조로다

150

As its character is lofty like the heaven, there is reservation even in its smile.
* From "Maehwasa Samcheop", a sijo by Widang Jeong In-Bo (1893 – 1950)

Pages 54 –

The print style: twenty four characters

Pages 54 – 56

구름 날고 섬 뜨고 하늘 푸른데
청옥빛 깊은 바다 산호당 속에
아름다운 비밀이 숨어 있으니
하얀 조개 꿈꾸는 금모랫가에
끝없이 밀려오는 물결 위로
나도 가고 배도 가고 바람도 간다

Clouds fly, islands float, and the sky is blue.
In a coral reef house under a deep green jade-colored sea,
Are beautiful secrets hidden.
On a golden shore where white seashells dream,
Over waves that flow in endlessly,
Do I, a boat and the wind go.
* "Bada sogok" (Small poem on the sea) by Kim Kwang-Seop (1905 – 1977)

Page 57

녹두밭에 앉지 마라
녹두꽃이 떨어지면
청포장수 울고 간다

Do not sit on green bean fields.
When flowers fall,
An iris selling merchant passes crying.
* From an old Korean folk song

Pages 58 –

The print style: small characters

Pages 58 – 61

내 고장 칠월은
청포도가 익어가는 시절
이 마을 전설이 주저리 주저리 열리고
먼 데 하늘이 꿈꾸며 알알이 들어와 박혀
하늘 밑 푸른 바다가 가슴을 열고
흰 돛단배가 곱게 밀려서 오면
내가 바라는 손님은 고달픈 몸으로
청포를 입고 찾아온다고 했으니
내 그를 맞아 이 포도를 따 먹으면
두 손을 함뿍 적셔도 좋으련
아이야 우리 식탁엔 은쟁반에
하이얀 모시 수건을 마련해 두렴
이육사

July in my home town,
It's the season of green grapes.
The legends of the village yield their fruit in clusters,
And the distant sky, dreaming, comes into each grape.
When the blue sea under the sky bares her hidden heart,
And a ship with white sails comes gently shoving,
The guest I await will visit with the blue robe over weary life.
If he shares the grapes on my table, I do not mind wetting my hands.
Boy, get ready on the tables a silver plate and a ramie napkin.
Lee Yuk-Sa
* "Cheongpodo" (Green grapes), a poem by Lee Yuk-Sa (1904 – 1944)

Page 62

삭풍은 나무 끝에 불고 명월은 눈 속에 찬데
만리변성에 일장검 짚고 서서
긴 파람 큰 한소리에 거칠 것이 없어라

Bitter winter wind blows over tree branches and a bright moon shines on the snow.
When I stand with a big sword in hand at a distant frontier castle,
Nothing stops my long whistle and loud shout.
* An old sijo by Kim Jong-Seo (1383 – 1453)

Page 63

내 벗이 몇이나 하니 수석과 송죽이라
동산에 달 오르니 긔 더욱 반갑고야
두어라 이 다섯 밖에 또 더하여 무엇하리

Name my friends, and I have water, stone, pine, and bamboo.
A moon rising over the top of a hill is also welcome.
Leave them. Beside these five, for what would I add more?
* From "Ohuhga" (My dear five friends), an old sijo by Gosan Yoon Seon-Do (1587 – 1671)

Page 64

청산은 어찌하여 만고에 프르르며
유수난 어찌하여 주야에 긏지 아니난고
우리도 그치지 말아 만고상청하리라

How can a green mountain remain evergreen?
How can water never pause running day and night?
We ought not to pause, either, to remain green forever.
* An old sijo by Toegye Lee Hwang (1502 – 1571)

Page 65

입 다문 꽃봉오리 무슨 말씀 지니신고
피어나 빈 것일진대 다문 대로 곕소서

What words does a flower bud keep unuttered in her closed mouth?
Perhaps she yearns to blossom up, so let her keep it closed as it is.
* From "Yip Damun Kot Bongori" (Flower bud with its

mouth closed), a poem by Nosan Lee Eun-Sang (1903 – 1982)

* *Sijo* is a genre of Hangeul poetry. A *sijo* consists of three lines, each typically containing fourteen to fifteen characters. The first and second lines are composed of three-four-three-four characters and the third three-five-four-three. This unique genre of Korean poetry has been popular for several hundred years.

Pages 86 –

The cursive style: six characters

Pages 86 – 87

아름다운 궁체
beautiful *Gungche*
노래의 메아리
echo of a song

Pages 88 – 89

옥에도 티 있다
Even jade has flaws.
단결은 힘이다
Unity is power.

Pages 90 – 91

단 솥에 물 붓기
pouring water in a hot pot
배 먹고 이 닦기
brushing teeth after eating a pear

Pages 92 – 93

따뜻한 봄 날씨
warm spring weather
찔레꽃 울타리
briar hedge

Pages 94 – 95

깨끗이 단정히
tidily and neatly
늘 푸른 소나무
evergreen pine tree

Pages 96 – 97

삶은 팥 볶은 콩
steamed red bean and fried soybean
장미꽃 목련화
rose and magnolia flower

Pages 98 – 99

뙤약볕 불바위
scorching sun and hot rock
끝없는 수평선
endless horizon

Pages 100 –

The cursive style: eight characters

Pages 100 – 101

태양은 또다시 뜬다
The sun rises again.
보름 삭는 생률이라
Uncooked chestnuts help cure boils.
* From "Nonggawollyeongga" (Monthly farm songs), an old *gasa* by Jeong Hak-Yu (1786 – 1855)

Pages 102 – 103

삽주 두릅 살찐 향채
spices enriched with atractylodes and spikenard
죽장 망혜 단표자로
with a bamboo cane and a gourd container only
* From "Nonggawollyeongga" (Monthly farm songs), an old *gasa* by Jeong Hak-Yu (1786 – 1855)

Pages 104 – 105

솟아나는 샘물처럼
like a rising fountain
깊은 산 속 뻐꾹 소리
cuckoo sound in a deep forest

Pages 106 – 107

초록 장옷 반물 치마
green feminine coat and deep indigo skirt
* From "Nonggawollyeongga" (Monthly farm songs), an old *gasa* by Jeong Hak-Yu (1786 – 1855)

푸른 하늘 흰 구름떼
blue sky and white clouds

Pages 108 – 109

넓은 들판 황금 물결
broad fields covered with golden tide of ripe crops
귀뚜라미 우는 달밤
cricket chirping moonlit night

Pages 110 – 111

발 없는 말 천리 간다
Words without feet travel a thousand miles.
한 술 밥에 배 부를까
Could a spoonful of meal make one full?

Pages 112 –

The cursive style: twelve characters

Pages 112 – 115

지리산 천왕봉을 언제 오를꼬
청학동 접어들어 길을 헤맬 제
칠불암 목탁 소리 다정도 하다
산차에 목 추기라 부르는구나
When could I climb Cheonwangbong of Jiri Mountain?

152

Entering Cheonghakdong, wandering lost,
I hear friendly sound of wood block hits from Chilbul Temple.
It's like calling me to join to sip mountain tea.
* From "Jogukgangsan" (Rivers and mountains of my motherland), a poem by Nosan Lee Eun-Sang (1903 – 1982)

Pages 116 – 117

남해는 번쩍이는 승리의 바다
The South Sea is a sea of shining triumph.
충무공 맹서하던 울도 한산도
Uldo and Hansando, where Admiral Lee Sun-Shin pledged victory

Pages 118 – 119

동짓달 열 아흐레 바람 찬 새벽
a windy dawn of the winter solstice moon
오늘은 이 민족의 부활절이다
Today is the day of our people's resurrection.

Pages 120 –

The cursive style: fifteen characters

Pages 120 – 121

사공이 많으면 배가 산으로 올라간다
If there are many boatmen, the boat goes up the mountain.
바쁘게 찧는 방아에도 손 늘 틈이 있다
Leisure may be found even during busy mill grinding.

Pages 122 – 123

될 성 부른 나무는 떡잎부터 알아본다
A promising tree is recognizable even from its cotyledons.
구슬이 서말이라도 꿰어야 보배니라
Three bushels of marble make treasure only when they are tied up.

Pages 124 – 126

빛나는 파란 잎새 파란 대공 하이얀 꽃
꽃마다 동글동글 옥비녀 꽂아 놓은 듯
이 아니 아름다우랴 이름 또한 옥잠화
Shining green leaves, green stems, and white flowers,
As if there's a round jade hairpin in every flower.
How could it not be beautiful? Its name, daylily.
* From "Okjamhwa" (Daylily), a sijo by Garam Lee Byeong-Ki (1891 – 1968)

Pages 127 – 129

돌바닥 맑은 샘아 돌 우는 듯 멈추어라
진흙밭 구정물에 행여 몸을 다칠세라
차라리 막힐지언정 흐려 흘러가리오
Clean fountain water springing from rock bottom!
Stop circling out.

Because your body might get hurt by muddy water,
You would rather like being blocked than getting dirty and flowing out.
* "Eoneu Maeum" (A mind), a sijo by Yukdang Choi Nam-Seon (1890 – 1957)

Pages 130 –

The cursive style: small characters

Pages 130 – 133

산 너머 남촌에는 누가 살길래
해마다 봄바람이 남으로 오네
꽃 피는 사월이면 진달래 향기
밀 익는 오월이면 보리 내음새
금잔디 넓은 벌엔 호랑나비떼
버들밭 실개천엔 종달새 노래
어느 것 한 가진들 실어 안 오리
남촌서 남풍 불 제 나는 좋데나
Who would live in a southern village over the mountain?
Wind comes from the south every year.
Every flowering April brings the scent of Azaleas,
Every wheat-ripening May, the barley scent.
Swallowtail butterflies fly on broad golden grass fields.
Larks sing over willow tree fields and brooklets.
Would any one of these not be carried by the wind?
When south wind blows from the southern village, I am delighted.
* From "San neomeo namchoneneun" (In a southern village over the mountain), a poem by Kim Dong-Hwan (1901 – 1958)

Pages 134 – 135

여럿이 가는 데 섞이면 병든 다리도 끌려간다
If many people go together, even the sick leg will be dragged along.
노동과 질서와 성실이 있는 곳에 기쁨도 있다.
Where labor, order, and sincerity prevail, joy is found, too.

Pages 136 – 139

내 죽으면 한 개 바위가 되리라
아예 애련에 물들지 않고
희로에 움직이지 않고
비와 바람에 깎이는 대로
억년 비정의 함묵에
안으로 안으로만 채찍질하여
드디어 생명도 망각하고
흐르는 구름 머언 원뢰
꿈꾸어도 노래하지 않고
두 쪽으로 깨뜨려져도
소리하지 않는
바위가 되리라
When I die, I will become a rock.
Never affected by love and pity
Never moved by joy and anger

But standing eroded by rain and wind
In heartless silence for hundreds of millions of years
Whipping inward over and over again
Finally forgetting life
Flying clouds and distant thunder
Dreaming yet not singing
Even broken into two pieces
Standing soundless
Will I become a rock.

* "Bawi" (Rock), a poem by Cheongma Yoo Chi-Hwan (1908 – 1967)

Page 140

삿갓에 도롱이 입고 세우 중에 호미 메고
산전을 흩매다가 녹음에 누웠으니
목동이 우양을 몰아 잠든 나를 깨와다

Wearing rain coat and umbrella, carrying a hoe in light rain
I lay down while weeding mountain fields.
A shepherd, guiding cows and sheep, woke me from sleep.

* An old *sijo* by Hanhwondang Kim Goeng-Pil (1454 – 1504)

Page 141

쓴 나물 데온 물이 고기도 곤맛이이
세초옥 좁은 줄이 긔 더욱 내 분이라
다만당 님 그린 탓으로 시람 계워 하노라

With bitter herbs and warm water, even meat tastes bitter.
A narrow thatched house is more than enough under my circumstances.
All my anxiety comes from missing my beloved, and I can hardly overcome it.

* An old *sijo* by Songgang Jeong Cheol (1536 – 1594)

Page 142

흰 구름 푸른 내는 골골이 잠겼는데
추상에 물든 단풍 꽃곤 더 좋아라
천공이 나를 위하여 뫼빛을 꾸며내도다

White clouds and blue streams are immersed in every valley.
Falling leaves colored by autumn frost are prettier than flowers.
For me has heaven created such mountain beauties.

* An old *sijo* by Nampa Kim Cheon-Taek (1680s – 1700s)

Page 143

두류산 양단수를 예 듯고 이제 보니
도화 뜬 맑은 물에 산영조차 잠겼어라
아희야 무릉이 어디오 나는 옌가 하노라

Having heard Yangdan Water in Duryu Mountain before and now do I see them,
Even mountain shadow is immersed in clean water

with peach flowers floating.
Boy, where is paradise? I assume it's here.

* An old *sijo* by Nammyeong Cho Sik (1501 – 1572)

* *Gasa* is another genre of Hangeul literature. A *gasa* has a basic rhythm of four-four characters and consists of multiple lines. Since there's no limit to the number of the basic unit in a poem, *gasa* works are often lengthy. This unique Hangeul verse has also been popular for several hundred years.

Pages 144 –

Examples of historical calligraphy: classic works by old masters

Page 144

Classic work by an old master / The print style / From "Women's four books"

어제녀사셔셔
그건곤의덕과음양의되큰디라
대개건은아비라일캇고곤은어미라일캇나니
하날과사람이곳한리라
일노써음양이고로하여야만믈이화하고
부뷔화하여야가되이나니
그런고로그나라희다슬며다스디못하미이
또한그집의가작하며가작디못하매잇나니라
쥬역에갈오대부뷔이신연후에부재잇고
부재이신연후군신이잇다하고
부재또갈오샤대굿치부부에진난다하시고
시견삼백편의그근본은곳이남며쥬문

The prelude of "Women's Four Books" published by royal authorities
The virtue of heaven and earth and the way yin and yang work are so great.
Since heaven is called the father and earth the mother, heaven and humans are indeed governed by a single principle.
Therefore, all creatures are made only when yin and yang work harmoniously.
And only when a husband and a wife are harmonious, their family works.
Hence, governing a country well or not depends on whether its constituent families are good.
According to the Classic of Changes, a husband and a wife are prerequisite to a father and a son, and a father and a son prerequisite to a king and his courtiers.
Confucius also says that the way in which an ideally ethical and capable man behaves begins with that of a husband and a wife.
The essence of three hundred poems of the Classic of Poetry lies with two Nams (Junam and Sonam), and King Mun of Zhou dynasty…

Classic work by an old master / The half cursive style / From "The list of bedclothes prepared for a princess' wedding"

남냥색왜듀핫금차다홍화사듀깃구
초록수화듀핫금차다홍의고듀깃구
남수화듀누비금차다홍화사듀깃구
보라듀누비금차남깃구
남듀쟁겹금차자력듀깃구
초록곱생초겹금차다홍화사듀깃구
자력토듀일필금차남깃구

(In modern Hangeul)
이불 물목
남양색(藍兩色) 왜주(倭紬, 일본명주)로 만든 솜이불감, 다홍색 화사주(花絲紬, 꽃명주실)로 만든 이불깃을 갖춤
초록물 화주(花紬, 꽃무늬 비단)로 만든 솜이불감, 다홍색 의고주로 만든 이불깃을 갖춤
남수화주로 만든 누비 이불감, 다홍색 화사주로 만든 이불깃을 갖춤
보라 색 비단 누비 이불감, 남색으로 만든 이불깃을 갖춤
남색 비단 쟁(재양(載陽)으로 풀을 먹인) 겹이불감, 자줏빛으로 만든 이불깃을 갖춤
초록 곱생초(가례에 쓰인 직물 이름) 겹이불감, 다홍색 화사주로 만든 이불깃을 갖춤
자적토 비단 일필 이불감, 남색으로 만든 이불깃을 갖춤

List of bedclothes
Cotton bedclothes covered with indigo colored Japanese silk, equipped with deep red floral silk thread collar
Cotton bedclothes covered with green colored floral silk, equipped with deep red archaic silk collar
Cotton bedclothes covered with indigo water colored floral silk, equipped with deep red floral silk thread collar
Cotton bedclothes covered with violet colored silk, equipped with indigo colored collar
Cotton bedclothes covered doubly with glue-pasted indigo colored silk, equipped with purple colored collar
Cotton bedclothes covered doubly with green *gopsaengcho*, equipped with deep red floral silk thread collar
Cotton bedclothes covered with purple red soil-colored silk, equipped with indigo colored collar

Glossary

but	brush
byeoru	a stone board on which Asian black ink is prepared by grinding ink stick for the purpose of calligraphy
calligraphy	the art of beautiful handwriting performed with a brush
cursive style	the style of writing in which characters are written by joining strokes in a flowing manner, generally to enable writing with rapidity
ending consonant	a consonant occupying the bottom position of a given Hangeul character
gasa	a genre of Hangeul literature (see p. 154)
gopsaengcho	name of textile used for preparing old Korean-style bedclothes
Gungche	palatial style; a classical style of Hangeul calligraphy primarily developed by royal and noble court women since the creation of Hangeul in the 15th century
half cursive style	a style of calligraphy in which the print and cursive forms are mixed. A character written in half cursive style can have either the print or cursive features of a vowel or consonant(s) or both. In the historical example of half cursive style (p. 145), characters are written mostly in the cursive style, but some such as '랴' and '구' are written in the print style. Moreover, characters such as '남' and '금' have features of both the cursive (thin connective line originating from the vowel) and print ('ㅁ') style. Thus, in characters written in half cursive style, the cursive style is only partially implemented.
Hangeul	the Korean alphabet. Invented by King Sejong (1453) of the Joseon dynasty (1392 – 1910), it is the official writing system of modern Korea.
Hanmun	Chinese characters; used as an official writing system until the end of the Joseon dynasty in Korea
hoek	calligraphic brush stroke
hwaseonji	traditional Asian paper used for calligraphy
initial consonant	a consonant occupying the head position of a given Hangeul character; also called a beginning consonant
meok	black solid ink (usually made into sticks) used to prepare *meokmul*. In calligraphy, it is ground on the surface of *byeoru* in the presence of water.
meokmul	Asian black ink used for brushwork in calligraphy
print style	a style of calligraphy in which characters are written clearly and separately stroke by stroke without joining them in a flowing manner; also termed regular style
sijo	a genre of Hangeul poems (see p. 152)
The March 1st Independence Movement	nationwide uprising and protest against Japanese rule on March 1, 1919 that occurred to regain the independence of Korea from Japanese occupation (1910 – 1945)

Index

Acknowledgments

I thank Bakok Choi Jae-Yeon (honorific titles omitted hereafter) for initially raising the possibility of translating 'Hangeul Calligraphy written by Gotdeul Lee Mi-Kyeong' into a foreign language, and Seulye Roh Ji-Yeon for the idea of translating it into English. Seulye also reviewed an initial version of the translation and advised on calligraphic knowledge. Critical review of an intermediate version was kindly provided by Hannwi Cho Ju-Yeon and Imcheon Lee Hwa-Ja, who gave insights into calligraphic methods. Crucially, translation of historical calligraphy works into modern Hangeul was provided by Sannae Park Jeong-Sook. Without the help from these distinguished members of the Galmul Hangeul Calligraphy Association, it would have been difficult to carry out translation into completion. Encouraging review by my elder sister Huinsaem Nam Woo-Jeong was also helpful. The most critical help at the last stage of translation was provided by Bommoe Lho Myong-Sook and her daughter Larissa Min, both residents of the United States, who edited the translation at the level of native English. Finally, the devotion of publisher Jung Young-Kook to the graphic work and frame establishment is highly appreciated.

Translator: Nam Young-Woo

Son of Gotdeul Lee Mi-Kyeong; graduated from Department of Agronomy of Seoul National University, Seoul, Korea (B. S., 1985; M. S., 1987); received Ph. D. from Purdue University, Indiana, U. S. A. (1994); served as Assistant and Associate Professor at School of Natural Science of Sogang University, Seoul, Korea (2000 - 2013). E-mail ywnam63@gmail.com.

Gotdeul Hangeul Calligraphy

First Published : November, 2024
Written by : Mi-Kyeong Lee
Editor & Translator : Young-Woo Nam
Publisher : Young-Kook Jung
Published by : Hak Won Publishing Co.
Address : No. 418, KS Tower 4F, 30 Beotkkot-ro 36-gil, Geumcheon-gu, Seoul 08511, Republic of Korea
Tel : +82-2-2135-8301   Fax : +82-2-584-9306

ISBN : 978-89-19-20597-6 (13710)
Price : 17,000 Won
Home page : http://www.hakwonsa.com

KB199034